Table of contents

MW01275083

Introduction

My name is Celia and I'm a 30-year-old mother to two girls: Jenny and Rosie. I'm married to Graham and we live a contented life in Devon. I won't say where exactly in Devon as it'll ruin the illusion of rolling hills and beautiful coastlines.

I wrote the majority of this book in April 2012 when my second baby, Rosie, arrived. I wrote chapters every few days to chart my experience and record the tips and tricks I picked up along the way.

I was left with a pretty comprehensive, diarised account of what it's like in the early months of dealing with a newborn and a toddler. So I decided to start blogging each chapter to see how popular the content was. The response was amazing so I decided to publish the most popular chapters in this ebook.

The result is a very personal account of how I coped with my toddler and my newborn. The book is also packed with empathy, tips and practical approaches to everyday challenges.

Furthermore, I interview several parents at various stages of the two under two experience. Their case studies are featured at the end of the book.

Being pregnant with your second baby is a daunting time, mainly because everyone delights in telling you how awful it's going to be, how you'll never sleep again etc. etc.

I really hope this book helps you to cope with the anxiety that naturally comes before welcoming baby number two.

And I also hope it shows you that it's not as bad as people would have you think.

I'd love to meet you. Visit me at www.twoundertwo.co.uk or say hello on Twitter @2_under_two. I'd also love to hear your honest thoughts and feedback on the book so it'd mean so much to me if you'd consider leaving a review on Amazon when you're finished.

Thank you - and congratulations on your growing family!

Introducing my two under two

Jenny, our eldest, has always been a handful. Pretty much from day one, she knew what she wanted and wasn't shy about demanding it (not least being a stubborn breech and having to be extracted through 'the sunroof').

It was only really in retrospect that I realised how difficult she was as a newborn.

She had terrible reflux and just wouldn't keep still – those coming in for snuggly baby cuddles quickly retreated upon being kicked in the delicates and covered in milky spew.

Rosie, our second daughter, is such a calm, serene baby. Some say this is down to the fact that babies are far more relaxed when in the care of someone with experience. I agree to a certain extent but mostly I just think I've been pretty fortunate.

Panic

During my second pregnancy, I got really sick of being told what a nightmare I was letting myself in for. Upon discovering I was mother to a toddler (20 months old when Rosie was born) and expecting number two, people seemed to take great pleasure in informing me that the next 20 years of my life would effectively be a write-off.

As a result, I spent the last few months of my pregnancy panicking about how I was going to cope. And it's not an overstatement to say I was simply terrified the night before I was due to take care of them on my own for the first time.

The reality

In reality, having two children under the age of two has been such a joy. Pretty much from day one (after recovering from my c-section, that is), managing the two of them became second nature and before long, I was enjoying a couple of hours off in the middle of the day while the two of them slept soundly. I was surprised at how naturally my abilities expanded so that I could care for two children.

I can pretty confidently guarantee that you'll soon feel the same, but a certain level of panic is a natural part of any growing family. I just wish I hadn't wasted so much time worrying about it and had enjoyed the latter stages of my pregnancy more.

I won't lie, there have been plenty of times when their needs have collided in dramatic fashion, but each time I've become more adept at quickly working out what needs to be done first. Poor Rosie quite often comes second, as Jenny's needs are far more vocal.

But I can honestly say that in those delicate first few months, there wasn't a second where I questioned my ability to cope. Really, I just got on with it.

I must admit I've been blessed with a baby who loves to sleep, so many parents reading this may want to throw bricks at my head.

However, please be pacified with the knowledge that my first baby woke up anywhere between 10 and 20 times a night for the first 8 months of her life. Also she had colic for the first 3 so I think I've paid my dues!

So...

Have faith in yourself.

Your experience with your first baby will stand you in good stead and I wouldn't mind betting you'll find caring for a newborn so much easier this time around. I'm not saying it's a total piece of cake, but it came as quite the surprise (and relief) to me that I was so relaxed and so assured in what I was doing.

So please trust that your natural instincts combined with your parental organisational skills will not let you down. I wish someone had told me that in advance.

The second pregnancy

Tip for the day: Get your newborn to nap in your/their bedroom during the day as soon as you can. It'll be nice and quiet for them and you and your toddler don't have to tiptoe around while they nap in the corner of your living room.

Symptom-wise, my second pregnancy was identical to my first. I was absolutely shattered throughout, wanted to eat great big piles of salt and went through boxes of cereal like they were going out of fashion.

But in terms of speed, my second pregnancy was nothing like my first. You will probably find the same.

The early days

For a start, the first 12 weeks whizzed by and before I knew it, I was having that precious first scan. I remember the first trimester of my first pregnancy being agony! Each day was like a week, each month like a year. I convinced myself daily that terrible things were going to happen and had regular nightmares about giving birth to a baby with a full set of teeth.

But being so busy with my demanding toddler made the first – and second – trimester of my second pregnancy go extremely quickly.

Conversely, my third trimester with Jenny went so fast I swear I got emotional whiplash. The weeks sped by as I remembered more and more stuff that I'd forgotten. And realised more and more stuff that I would no longer be able to do once my baby arrived.

A lot of people told me my second pregnancy would go much more quickly and I would agree wholeheartedly – until 30 weeks.

The last leg

30 weeks onwards was a struggle through mud for me, not least because I had a very sore pelvis and a very energetic Jenny. It was at 30 weeks that I started greedily accepting all the offers of help I had, until that point, graciously refused.

My mother-in-law flew down from Scotland to help out and I don't know what I would've done without her. She would take Jenny to the park for hours on end and I would climb into bed, often not re-emerging until the following morning.

Send for help

I was very lucky to have so much help and I would urge anyone in the same situation to grab it with both hands. If you don't have family or friends nearby to help, consider a nursery or a childminder if you haven't already. Or if you have, try stepping up the hours if you can afford it. You may even find that there are local organisations who send out volunteers to help people in your situation.

I felt very guilty at first when Jenny was receiving all this care from other people but it made me happier for the time I was with her and preserved my energy.

Most people can track down some form of help so I would encourage you to take full advantage of it. People don't offer unless they mean it, so go ahead and accept any and all help.

I appreciate that not everyone has family and friends around who can help. If you're in this position, don't feel guilty about popping your toddler in front of a film if you need to lie down for 10 minutes. You need your rest now more than ever, and your toddler won't mind in the slightest.

Keep active

Having said the above, staying active on a regular basis is essential for so many reasons. Your health, your toddler's happiness and most likely your newborn's delivery will all receive a positive boost if you can get out in the fresh air as much as possible. Plus it'll really help you to stay sane - there's nothing worse than cabin fever when you're pregnant and encumbered with an energetic toddler.

Don't push yourself too hard, but get to the park, walk to the shop or even take a few turns around your garden if you have one.

But stay close to the house, just in case!

After the arrival

Although pregnancy totally wiped me out, I found that a few weeks after Rosie arrived, I experienced a real surge of energy. I think having been so weighed down for such a long time, I forgot what it was like to have normal energy levels.

Once I'd recovered from the caesarean, I was like a new woman – even with the sleep deprivation. I was getting more done than I ever expected and was pleased that it wasn't the struggle I was expecting.

I really hope that your experience is the same, and that you find new levels of energy once you're no longer carrying around that huge baby bump!

But if you don't, try not to worry. It's a learning curve for your whole family and everyone will adapt at their own pace.

Jealousy and preparing your toddler

Tip for the day: If you don't already have one, invest in a quality, musical mobile to go above the cot. This is a great place for your newborn to unwind and kick out the last of their energy away from a potential toddler trampling.

The thing I was most worried about when Rosie arrived was Jenny getting jealous of all the attention her new sister was receiving. She'd also been passed around the extended family somewhat in the last weeks of my pregnancy when I wasn't much use to anyone, let alone a very needy toddler.

Dealing with jealousy

There are countless things you can do to ensure that your toddler doesn't become too jealous of your new arrival, many of which we employed. We have been very lucky with our two and Jenny has really taken to her little sister (despite her enthusiastic 'cuddles' which can get a bit dramatic).

Before Rosie arrived, we talked to Jenny a lot about what was to come. We didn't want her thinking that 'the baby' was something we only talked to other adults about. However we steered very clear of telling her that she was going to get a fun new playmate; I think this only serves to disappoint toddlers when they discover that this 'fun new playmate' pretty much just poos, sleeps and eats. Then poos again.

We made sure she understood that I was growing a baby and encouraged her to cuddle and kiss my belly lots. We also practised being gentle and not grabbing/poking/smacking. We bought her a doll for Christmas which was useful for practising gentle affection.

Whatever you do, just take it at a gentle pace and try not to worry too much. Toddlers are exceptionally talented at picking up on their parents' anxiety so if you don't panic, chances are neither will they.

Managing jealousy

Since Rosie's arrival, I have been very careful to be as fair as possible to Jenny. It can be tempting to make her wait for things while I sort her little sister out. After all, our natural urges all scream at us to protect our newborn child. But I generally find that letting Rosie wait creates far fewer meltdowns. Of course, if Rosie's screaming her head off I go to her first but usually I can sort out whatever Jenny needs beforehand. As long as there's a tangible balance, your toddler shouldn't feel too put out if they don't always come first.

I also make a point of telling Rosie that she has to wait so that Jenny gets some audible confirmation that she's still just as important. I started doing this around week four as I noticed myself saying to Jenny: 'In a minute, you'll just have to wait' an awful lot, which can't be easy on a sensitive toddler who's used to having Mummy all to herself.

Hearing stuff like: 'Just a second Rosie, Mummy's going to read your sister a story then we'll change your nappy' seems to really puff Jenny up and remind her that she's still important. Of course, your newborn has no idea what you're banging on about and just gazes gummily up at you. So everyone's a winner!

You know your toddler best and some things may work better than others. Be sure to be patient with yourself and your toddler, it'll be a steep old learning curve but your instincts will give you the nod if things are going a little off balance.

I find it useful (and refreshing) to stop and put myself in Jenny's shoes when I'm struggling. Rather than treating her like a little adult who should understand everything, I try to remind myself often to be more sympathetic and patient with things that she doesn't yet understand about having a younger sibling. After all, she's still really just a baby herself.

Other things you could try

There is loads of advice out there for coping with jealousy. I did a ridiculous amount of web-trawling so here are some of the best tips I picked out:

- Have a toy ready to give your toddler 'from the baby'. When Jenny arrived, we bought a book of stories for her older half-sister and they still love reading it together.
- When your toddler first meets the baby, make sure your arms are free for cuddles. If s/he arrives to find their rightful place has been reassigned, you're more likely to get off on the wrong foot.
- Make any necessary changes to your toddler's routine in advance (with beds especially). We didn't do this and fortunately the two of

them fit in with each other well but it took some work initially.

- Use the 'Candle' approach – light one candle to represent you, then light another from it. Tell your toddler this is you giving all of your love to your partner when you met. Then using the two candles, light another one for your toddler and explain how love is magic and can multiply. Then you can light the baby's candle together. We couldn't do this with Jenny as she would've set fire to the house… But it's a lovely sentiment nonetheless if you can get it past health and safety. Perhaps try it with tap water flowing into cups!

- Do everything you can to get your newborn (as soon as possible) to smile at your toddler. They'll probably do this anyway. Jenny absolutely loves it when Rosie smiles at her. Lots of tickles under the chin, or just try to catch your baby when they're feeling a bit windy!

- Make sure you and your toddler get a significant chunk of time together every single day. This should be manageable while your newborn is napping but if you have trouble finding the time, see if someone can babysit for an hour while you take your toddler to the park or just for a walk. Even just 10 minutes of stories on the sofa will mean the world to them.

- Having a special drawer, cupboard or plastic toybox for your toddler to house their 'special things'. This makes them feel important and that they still have a place in the house. And it keeps things out of their sibling's reach. You can label their drawer with stickers which your toddler will love to help with. When your new baby gets older, they can have a drawer too. Your toddler will like putting toys in the draw to keep them safe from their dribbly sibling.

Any small efforts you make to avoid jealousy in these early stages will pay off big time in the long run. Don't feel like you have to do everything to ensure your toddler doesn't experience even the slightest jolt of envy: this is unavoidable and is a good life lesson.

The best you can do is manage the frequency of these episodes; this way your children are far more likely to get off to the best start.

Breastfeeding

Tip for the day: *This 'sleep when the baby sleeps' thing just doesn't fly when you have a toddler to look after as well. My advice to a brand new mother of two under two is to go to bed whenever you get them both down for the night – ideally around 7pm. Personally, I find that 12 hours of sleep that's broken several times is far better than 6-7hrs broken once or twice.*

I'm not going to go into the details of breastfeeding or bore you with my story. It's a hugely personal matter and everyone's experience is completely different.

What's important is to figure out a way to make breastfeeding work for you if that's how you've chosen to feed your newborn. It can be a juggle at first, but getting prepared is key to overall breastfeeding success. You'll find that the first few weeks are filled with you trying to find your own natural rhythm, but there are certainly ways in which you can get there without too much disruption.

Finding time

If you choose/are able to breastfeed, the hardest part is that the onus is on you to do the feeding, 24/7. And during those early weeks when your newborn is feeding non-stop to spike your supply, it would take a pretty tough little toddler not to be bothered by it.

So it's important to take the time to consider their feelings about all this. After all, they've spent the past 18 months or so being the absolute centre of your world. Suddenly seeing another little person attached to you is going to be hard for them to deal with.

Emotionally, everyone deals with the difficulties of breastfeeding differently. But on a practical level, the following things I learnt might be helpful to others:

- This might not be so easy at first, but try to give your toddler a little bit of warning before you start a feed. You can give them some limited activity choices to pick from and set it up in preparation.
- You probably have a stair gate or two already, but see if you can pick up a spare one for your living room door (or for whichever room

you'll be doing the majority of your feeding in). You'll be pretty immobile while you feed so it'll be mighty helpful to keep your toddler contained in the same room as you. Try not to draw their attention to the gate: just make it a natural part of coming in and out of the room.

• Buy a special feeding pillow. It looks a bit like an airline pillow and I found it so helpful for achieving a comfortable feeding position. If you're comfortable, you're more likely to be able to give your toddler some attention while your baby is feeding.

• Have a 'feeding box' full of toys that only comes out when your feeding station does. You can switch the contents every now and again, putting in fresh supplies or digging out old toys that haven't seen the light of day for a while. Lego is particularly useful for occupying little hands. And pop along to your local pound or charity shop (or send your partner). Stock up your cupboards with a few fun little surprises to throw in if you're having a particularly bad day.

• It may not be possible straight away, but try to master feeding with one arm free. This arm can be wrapped around your toddler's shoulders while you read books together. This took me a good month to master.

• Go on, just put the telly on! If you don't generally rely on it for entertainment, the novelty will buy you some time. Or, if your toddler has a favourite programme/character, use the web to find videos. We spent a lot of time watching music videos and also digging out old videos of Jenny as a baby.

• Depending on your toddler's age, buy a magazine with stickers for them to play with while you nurse. Be prepared for these to be applied to your table/sofa/breast/newborn.

• If you don't have one already, buy a water-based drawing mat. Your toddler can doodle away without you having to jump up suddenly to stop them drawing on the walls. They come with their own pens but a covered cup of water and a brush can be much more fun.

• If you can learn to nurse your newborn in a sling, it'll make those growth spurts so much easier. There are good support videos online that will show you how to do this. Using a sling while you nurse keeps your arms and hands free to tend to your toddler's needs and even get on with a few household chores.

• If you're not tandem nursing, offer your toddler some expressed milk in a cup if they're really interested. Most toddlers (providing they're long since weaned from the breast) will usually lose interest as soon as they know it's not exclusively for their sibling.

- Again, this is age dependent, but games like 'I Spy' and 'Simon Says' will keep your toddler entertained. Let them choose their favourite game each time, but be sure to limit the choices to avoid having to say 'no'.
- Have a look through your toddler's baby album together while you feed, especially if you have photos of them nursing.
- Try to coordinate your toddler's meals with feeds where possible. If they're entertained with a tray of food, they're less likely to be pulling at your sleeve for attention.
- When your baby has finished nursing, involve your toddler with trying to get any burps out. This is a good opportunity to reinforce gentle touch as well.
- Ask your toddler to bring you things, even if you don't need them. Muslins, remote controls, drinks – they'll love being Mummy's Little Helper, so make a big fuss of them. Get a sticker chart to reward these little efforts.

A lot of these tricks can also be employed if you're bottle feeding and I still use many of them myself.

Successfully breastfeeding your newborn is totally achievable. People may like to tell you it's impossible when you have a toddler to run around after but don't listen. You just need to be super-organised and pretty creative. And, above all, patient with yourself, your toddler and your newborn.

If you're worried about your toddler becoming jealous, try to balance the attention so that your toddler gets some quality one-on-one time with you while your newborn is napping or otherwise engaged. Spend lots of time reading books together and chatting while they enjoy their food, so that they feel like they're getting similar levels of attention. If your toddler enjoys a cup or beaker of milk before bed, use this time to have lovely cuddles.

And remember that, as with everything else, you'll be a master at managing this in no time - so give yourself a break if it doesn't go smoothly straight away.

Two lots of needs, one pair of hands

Tip for the day: *If using expressed or formula milk, you can end up spending a criminal amount of money on baby bottles but, providing you don't have a colicky baby, you may well find that good old supermarket bottles are absolutely fine. Plus they're cheap enough to warrant buying new ones each month.*

It's a regular occurrence that your toddler needs something at the exact point that your newborn wants you too. Today Jenny was hopping from foot to foot waiting for her breakfast while Rosie was crying for her bottle.

What do we do in classic two under two situations like these?

Give yourself a break

First of all I always remind myself that I'm human and only capable of so much. And getting in a flap and clumsily trying to manage both things at once only upsets us all.

Instead of seeing to these clashing needs in a manner that suits no one and irritates everyone, try to divert your little ones to buy yourself some time.

If your toddler is hungry, hand them a small snack while you sort out your newborn. We use handfuls of cereal spread out on the highchair tray when we need to buy a few minutes. They're quick to grab and easy to clean up. Picking them up one by one takes time and she loves pushing them around, making patterns and counting. We also give her a dolly and a bib so she can pretend to feed her.

If you have a play mat, rocker, bouncer, vibrating chair or similar for your baby, try popping them on/in there for a couple of minutes while you placate your toddler, all the while keeping yourself in the sights of your baby. Moving/musical mobiles are the best for this - they can keep little eyes occupied for a few minutes while you address something else. Once your baby has a good grip, you can attach several rattles and toys nearby for them to play with.

Best of all, as mentioned, getting your toddler involved is a trick you'll employ again and again. Asking them to hand you a wipe or a nappy bag makes them feel important and also helps them to bond with their sibling.

Or, if your newborn is having a really hard time, give your toddler a pile of washing to take out of the basket and put in the machine. I use this one all the time!

Who comes first?

As a general rule, I tend to sort Jenny out first, as many recommend. After all, your little newborn is far more likely to forget they've been kept waiting and they aren't capable of jealousy.

Of course, sometimes I have to see to Rosie first. Either the situation demands it or I'm trying to achieve more of a balance. It wouldn't do to always put Jenny first. As long as I keep up a commentary for her benefit, she's usually fine with waiting.

Very few situations are so pressing that they can't wait for a few minutes. And learning to wait for their turn is one of the best life skills you can provide for your children.

For your part, learning to juggle both of their needs is a skill at which you will quickly become a master, trust me.

And if you get it a little bit wrong sometimes, so what? Be kind to yourself, it happens.

Handling night feeds

Tip for the day: *If you get to bed early enough the night before, getting up with your newborn is a very good idea. It's tempting to give them a bottle and fall back to sleep for an hour or so but getting yourself up, showered and freshened can set you on a good course for a successful day with both of your babies.*

For the first few weeks, it was down to me solely to feed Rosie at night as I was breastfeeding. This naturally took its toll. Dealing with a toddler is hard enough sometimes even with a good night's sleep behind you.

Exhaustion is one of those unavoidable things about having two young children. About having any number of young children.

It's going to happen sometimes and it's going to be a pain in the neck. But with enough support and the occasional night off (where possible), you will get through it.

Co-sleeping

We didn't co-sleep with Jenny at all. I'm not against it in the slightest; I just never felt the need. But this time around, we've turned to co-sleeping on a number of occasions when Rosie has been restless.

If you feel comfortable doing so, many new parents co-sleep with their baby. Do your research first (ignore all the scaremongering – it's perfectly safe when you stick to the rules) so that you feel really confident.

Co-sleeping is great particularly if you're breastfeeding as you don't have to get out of bed. If you're bottle feeding, you can have all the bits you need close at hand for minimum disruption. We took a flask of hot water upstairs with us so we could warm bottles easily without having to trudge down to the kitchen in the early hours.

Co-sleeping may be a tricky habit to break further down the line, but worry about that when it comes. Right now, it's more important to get that much-needed rest.

Acceptance

Feeding your baby during the night is up there with the most challenging aspects of having a newborn. But when it's your first, you can catch up on sleep during the following day. That option's out of the window when you have a full-time day job with your toddler.

It's a matter of accepting you'll have broken sleep for the first six months at least. Then if your baby starts sleeping through sooner, it's a happy bonus.

Try to remember: what's six months out of a whole lifetime? It doesn't always help (especially if you're really shattered) but it's held me back from a full-on tantrum on a number of occasions.

Your baby will almost certainly start sleeping for longer periods once they're weaned so you can hang on to that when you're really struggling.

Stock up when you can

I find that one unbroken night can help revive me after a long stint of doing the night feeds. After just one night off, I am happy to carry on for a good few days unassisted.

If you have a supportive partner or a relative who can come to stay, ask them to take over the night feeds for one night a week (or more if they offer!). You'll be amazed at the renewed energy it gives you.

And, as you know, it's all about energy when you're the primary carer of a toddler.

Staying sane

Tip for the day: Play a quiet song to your newborn while giving the last bottle of the day, and use the same song nightly. Choose something you can hum if you're ever caught short without your music player. It'll help signal to them that it's night time and a long sleep is coming next.

My saving grace since Rosie came along has been routine and keeping everything in order.

What? You? No!

As my family and old friends will agree, it's not in my nature to be organised and tidy. I have had to learn how to be more prepared than the most avid scout.

Before I had children, if there was washing in the sink, it'd stay there until it started to develop its own ecosystem. If there was laundry in the basket, the socks were more likely to crawl out of their own accord than be slung in the machine by yours truly.

Jenny's arrival made me slightly more organised but still not what you would call house proud. However now that we have two under two I've developed a not unhealthy addiction to being organised and keeping things tidy. Ish.

I'm not up at 2am scrubbing the skirting boards or anything but I will always make sure the house is relatively tidy by the end of the day so that I don't have to worry about it in the morning. The change bag is usually packed with everything I might need and the washing is put away so that there are plenty of clothes for the girls (and us) in the morning.

Early days

Of course, the first few weeks were a write-off and we succumbed to disorder and piles of washing as any new parents must. But the key was getting Rosie into a routine that fitted ours – or, more to the point, Jenny's.

When Jenny was tiny, I suffered a little bit of depression. Whether it was post-natal depression or not, I don't know. All I know is I felt rotten. I couldn't understand how other mothers were coping so well; I felt convinced that Jenny hated me and just couldn't get it together to leave the house.

It took a few weeks and a lot of tears before I took matters into hand (I've always been quite good at yanking myself out of gloomy moods – and that's why I'm not sure I had PND as I know it's not so easy to do that) and started forcing myself to get out of the house more. I went to baby groups, joined a baby massage group (which was great for bonding and relieving Jenny's colic) and made sure I got out at least once a day.

I started doing the same pretty early on this time around. Getting out of the house with two under two is not easy and it takes some getting used to, but I make myself do it several times a week. If I didn't, we'd all go potty.

Easy outings

If you aren't in the mood for tackling a full-on outing, try strapping them both into the car and going for a drive. If it's a warm day, crack the windows to get some fresh air circulating.

I give Jenny plenty of toys (soft, as they usually get launched around the car) and make sure Rosie's well fed and due for a nap.

Invest in some storytime or song CDs (several – the same one over and over again will send you potty). These can be picked up for next to nothing at charity or pound shops.

Don't punish yourself

Above all else, the best tip I ever received for staying sane was to lower my expectations. The stuff I used to achieve in a day became immediately impossible once I was juggling two children. But of course, I still tried to do it.

That lasted all of a couple of weeks and now I'm happy if I manage to hang the washing out before night falls (I don't always remember to get it back in again).

Some days are far more productive than others but it all depends on your energy levels and how the kids are doing. Teething, feeding, naps and general mood can have a huge impact on what you can get done in a day.

Try to be kind to yourself and adjust your expectations according to your new situation. Trust me, most people will think you're amazing if you manage to shower twice a week.

Transport options

Tip for the day: Change your newborn and toddler at the same time where possible. If you don't, you may end up feeling like all you've dealt with is nappies all day. And, if you're like me, it erases the possibility of forgetting to do one until it's hanging around their knees (sorry Jenny).

We have pretty much every child transport option known to man: a behemoth double buggy, a lightweight stroller, a not-so-lightweight stroller, a car seat, a sling, a toddler backpack and a Baby Bjorn baby carrier.

The one thing we decided against was a buggy board. These look like an absolutely brilliant idea but I decided Jenny was too young. A bit of research suggested that they're preferable when your toddler can go some considerable distances without getting tired.

It's important to remember that straight away, you'll be doing a wonderful job if you just get out once a week with your toddler and newborn.

As time marches on, you'll get better at organising and accomplishing outings with minimal fuss. Your baby's routine will become more predictable and you'll have bigger windows for getting out and about.

Your toddler won't mind staying in a bit more as long as you make things interesting at home but I wouldn't mind betting you'll be climbing the walls before too long. This will drive you to get to grips with leaving the house more often with your tribe.

Get out!

You will also soon find that being out of the house makes the time go a lot faster. There's nothing worse than being stuck at home with a bored toddler, clock-watching and getting on each other's nerves. I've known afternoons that have felt a year long.

Personally, I find that by far the most suitable option when we're out and about is putting the little one in the baby carrier and the toddler in a stroller. This way you don't take up any more space than you did with just the one child (though you will probably still argue with grumpy geriatrics like I have done) and the littlest baby will love being so close to you and probably sleep soundly for the majority of your outing.

Note: during those early weeks where the baby's head is lolling around, it's handy to use a few soft muslins rolled up to buffer their head if you're using a baby carrier.

When your baby gets older (6 months plus), your toddler should be able to cope with short outings on foot, so you can pop your baby in the stroller.

Invest in some reins for your toddler if (like me) you have an escape artist. They will be met with disgust but you don't have to use them, just dangle them as a possibility if your toddler doesn't stay close.

Achievable outings

Getting out of the house with two will seem like such a huge effort when you first try it. But, as I've mentioned, being organised in advance makes everything so much more manageable.

Making sure the nappy bag is well stocked the night before and preparing any feeds in advance (a dispenser is a must if you're using formula) by washing up and sterilising bottles makes your life so much easier.

It's also a life-saver to have a list of your essentials somewhere in eyeshot so that you can do a last-minute check. You don't want to be stuck somewhere with an impossibly snotty toddler and no wet wipes.

If you're going somewhere where your toddler is going to want to run around (for example the local park), having your newborn in a carrier is very handy for following them. However, if you're heading somewhere safer (an indoor play area or a friend's garden), you can always lay your newborn down in the toddler's stroller (providing it reclines) to have a nap while you muck about with your older child.

Soft play areas

Yesterday we headed to our local soft play area as it has been chucking down with rain for days. For a trip such as this, you only need the car seat for your newborn. Your toddler doesn't need somewhere to rest but you'll be glad of the safe seat for your baby while you sit and relax. With any luck, they'll fall asleep in there and you can enjoy mucking about with your toddler.

This trip was all going quite well until Jenny had a little puke in the ball pit. I managed a decent clean-up operation with wipes but got some pretty disgusted looks from other parents.

Sometimes it doesn't matter how prepared you are, things can't always go smoothly. But as long as you keep a sense of humour, it's onwards and upwards.

Managing your routine in the mornings

Tip for the day: *If you're dealing with your newborn and have a toddler who can be a little fussy about food, there isn't always enough time in the day to make sure they're getting enough nutrition. Try blending up a vitamin-rich smoothie and giving it to your toddler in a cup with a straw. The excitement of a new drink and a colourful straw will almost certainly make sure they finish the lot.*

Being up and at 'em first thing is not an inherent quality of mine.

I used to get up at 7.55am to leave for work at 8. I would wash my hair the night before, forego breakfast and head out fresh-faced. Of course, I was in my early twenties then and even with a monster hangover, I still managed to look presentable without too much effort. How I wish that were still the case!

Organisation

As I've mentioned, being organised plays a huge part in making the morning routine easy with our two under two. Generally we get up at around 7 and fortunately, Jenny doesn't usually rise until half past at the earliest. If she does decide to wake earlier, we shut the upper stairgate and let her play around upstairs while we get ready. One of us keeps an eye on her and the other sorts Rosie out.

Getting Rosie fed and changed before we see to Jenny makes everything so much easier. And Jenny doesn't seem to mind this routine. Doing things this way around usually means Graham and I can be washed and ready for the day with Rosie happy to kick around on her play gym or sit in her bouncer while we all have breakfast together.

Expect the unexpected

Of course, it doesn't always go smoothly; sometimes Rosie decides to wake up at 5am which throws things off. But generally we try to stick to this routine, mainly because it's manageable even if one of us is unavailable first thing. If Graham has to leave early for work, I can usually handle the morning routine alone.

Once breakfast is done and the kitchen has been spruced a little while Jenny flings porridge at us, we go and play in the living room or garden (weather permitting) until Rosie's nap is due.

She usually lies on her play gym and we both mess around trying to make her laugh for a while. When Jenny gets bored of that we place the gym safely in the travel cot so Rosie can continue to kick about without being at risk of a trampling.

Quality time for your toddler

Once Rosie is tucked up for her first nap of the day, Jenny and I have uninterrupted play time. I usually have an activity up my sleeve for this part of the day so that we make the most of it. It could be singing, housework, learning numbers or just good old-fashioned drawing/colouring.

Handling the morning routine this way leaves the afternoons free for outings. As Jenny still usually naps before lunch, the afternoons are pretty long. This means we definitely need to get out of the house to avoid going stir crazy.

You can use their synchronised lunchtime naps to organise everything you'll need during your trip. You can also prepare lunch for your toddler. Hopefully there'll still be half an hour in the routine for a bit of you time, too.

Discipline

Tip for the day: Always keep some sweets/a treat in the change bag for any older siblings. A super distraction when the younger demands feeding while you're out and about.

As I've mentioned, Jenny has always been a very wilful character. Partly, I'm glad because it'll be an asset when she's older but a wilful toddler is quite a handful at times, as those in the know will agree.

The best advice I ever received about discipline when number two came along was not to change a single thing. However you've been managing discipline beforehand, make sure you stick to it (unless of course it's failing miserably – but the time for a rehash is not when you've just brought an attention-stealer home from the hospital – give it a few weeks).

Consistency is everything

When Rosie arrived it became even more of a challenge to stay on the ball and make sure Jenny was still kept in hand, without her feeling constantly admonished while her little sister received all the coos and kisses. Tiredness and naughty behaviour makes for ugly moods and over-reactions - discipline is king.

A recent meltdown came about because Jenny wanted ice cream for breakfast. Don't we all? But I had to be the tough, boring mummy and insist on porridge. Of course, once the idea of ice cream was in her head, I might as well have served up a colossal steaming cow pat. She threw the whole lot on the floor.

At times like these, I really struggle to keep my cool. As if I don't have enough to do without scrubbing porridge from the grouting? But I knew I had to do what I always do.

Do it your way

Discipline is a sensitive area and everyone has their own approach, which must be respected. I'm not firmly in any camp when it comes to discipline techniques and I am certainly not about to tell you how you should be doing it.

In my opinion, it doesn't matter if you use the naughty step, the 'calm down' chair or the 'devil child' cupboard under the stairs (kidding). Just as long as you do something, and stick to it.

The key is consistency. As long as your child knows how you are going to discipline if they start to really push it, I'd say you're on the right tracks. If one day you scream and the next you completely ignore them, their confusion will only make matters much worse.

How I do it

When Jenny starts to mess about pushing boundaries and trying to wind me up, it can be very hard to stay calm. But staying calm is the most important part of our approach to discipline. A firm voice can get quite loud without turning into shouting – and a firm voice has always put the fear of God into me far more than screaming ever could.

I have my 'Mummy voice' that she knows really means business. Usually a firm 'No' will do the trick. If it doesn't, she gets a warning.

If she continues to misbehave she has to go and sit on the stairs until she calms down. I time it so she stays for at least one minute. I tell her that she has to stay there until she calms down, and that I'll be waiting to play when she's in a better mood but she needs to get her frustration out first.

While she's on the step, I busy myself going back and forth. I don't pay her any attention, just faff about while keeping an eye on her.

When she's definitely calmed down and served some time, I get down to her level, ask if she's 'Okay now' and almost always I get: 'Okay now, Mummy' in response. Then we have a hug and normal play resumes – which lets her know that things don't change just because she's been a little monkey. I still love her and am not going to hold a grudge when the discipline is finished. It sounds silly but I've seen it alarmingly often: parents remaining in a strop long after their child's has finished. Lead by example!

It's pretty much the naughty step approach and I certainly don't claim to have invented it. It gets used maybe a couple of times a week. More often than that and I fear it'd lose its clout.

Picking your battles

With any child - and with Jenny in particular - you've really got to learn to pick your battles. If you start popping them on the stairs every time they go against your wishes, you wouldn't get much else done. And it'd lose its clout.

You don't need a hard and fast list of things that are okay and things that aren't, just use your judgement and you will be fine.

The main area where you have to be super-careful about discipline is when your baby is involved. If your toddler hits your baby, naturally you want to come down hard on them. But equally you don't want to create jealousy. Use your judgement – be firm but fair.

And if your baby accidentally kicks your toddler (as they do with their little excited legs sometimes), make sure you give them a firm 'You mustn't kick your brother/sister'. Try to keep the rules them same for both of them as much as you can.

Dividing your attention

Tip for the day: If your baby is weaned and is teething, try freezing slices of banana for a few hours. They go squishy again really quickly and the cold will do wonders for your baby's grizzling.

A big challenge that's reared its head in parenting two under two is making sure they both get enough of my attention. Then there's the attention that needs to be given to housework, organisation and general bits and pieces that need to get done during the day.

Rosie takes great delight in just half an hour here and there of smiles and tickles before wanting to go off to bed again, so she's easily pleased. This kind of attention goes a long way with a newborn and can be done with your toddler alongside (until they get bored and start trying to poke their sibling in the eye). I also make sure Rosie and I get some quality time in the evenings after her sister has gone to bed by putting her to bed a little later.

It was making sure that Jenny's needs were fulfilled that I struggled with initially.

Don't forget to play!

At first, I was just so happy that I was juggling two young children without massive incident.

But I realised quickly that when Rosie was sleeping, rather than getting in some quality time with Jenny, I was turning my hand to the housework that had piled up.

It can be so tempting to attack that mountain of washing up, tidy a little bit as you go or do some dusting while your toddler plays. But it's important to remember that if they feel like they're being ignored (even though you've always got an eye on them), they will start to play up for your attention.

They may not always want you down at their level, you know your toddler best so it's your call. If they're clearly deeply involved in something, your sudden interference might upset their concentration. Just sit quietly nearby (have a cuppa!) and offer some praise if they happen to look up. They'll be thrilled that you're interested in what they're doing.

On the other hand, if they're flitting from toy to toy and not really getting involved in anything in particular, try getting down a jigsaw or a book and see if they are interested. That one-on-one time will mean a lot to both of you.

Arranging your time

I try to organise things so that I can spend some quality time with Jenny every day. Because she's so independent, she will happily play for a while on her own. But she still craves her parents' attention like any other toddler; I find that if I don't sit with her and read or play for at least an hour or two every day, she really picks up on it.

Your playtime armoury

It's handy to have a supply of fun games and activities on hand for these times. We have drawing materials, colouring books, Play-Doh, jigsaws, stuffed toys and imaginary play items such as tea sets and a play oven. Noisy toys are Jenny's favourite but I keep them in a high cupboard as I can only stand the noise for so long. Especially when she sets them all off at once…

But there's always stuff to be done too and it can get you down if you feel like you're achieving absolutely nothing in the day. The temptation when that happens is to do it in the evening when you should be relaxing and enjoying some time to yourself.

The balancing act

Achieving a healthy balance of work and play doesn't come easily but you'll get there. Don't beat yourself up if it takes some getting used to. Some days you might reach 5pm still in your pyjamas, and that's perfectly okay. Others you might have a tidy living room, dinner on the stove and freshly-washed hair.

For any amount of time I spend doing the washing up, sorting the laundry, answering emails (I run a business) etc. I make sure there's a balanced period that I spend with Jenny. I don't always play with her necessarily as that seems to annoy her if she's concentrating. I didn't get that at first, but sometimes she just wants to get on with what she's doing but know that I'm watching. I make sure that I'm on hand and undistracted if she wants anything from me, even if it's just a bit of praise. Her sister's arrival seems to have increased her need for positive reinforcement.

It's elementary when you sit and think about it – but it was a couple of months before I had the time to do that. When Rosie gets a little older I'm sure I'll have to revisit how I divide my time but I'll cross that bridge when I come to it. And probably employ a cleaner.

Putting your toddler in nursery

Tip for the day: If you have the space, get hold of a big cardboard box for your living room. Turning it into a little house (making curtains, decorating the outside with crayons etc.) will make a great project for you and your toddler and when your baby is a little bigger, they can play together in there. While you nurse/feed your baby, your toddler can sit in their house feeding their dollies.

Before Rosie was born and when Jenny was about 18 months old, we decided to try putting her in nursery for one afternoon a week. It was a precursor to me being physically useless at the end of my pregnancy and being super busy when the baby arrived.

Choosing a nursery

Unfortunately, the first one we tried didn't work out (this was mostly my fault as I should've done more research – I pretty much just went with the first available nursery I found). Jenny really didn't seem happy there and I was never comfortable leaving her. At first I thought this was just standard anxiety on both of our parts but as the weeks wore on, I realised it was time to trust my instincts.

I spent a couple of weeks researching (OFSTED reports can be found online) and asking around. I enquired at the toddler group we attend and also asked plenty of mum friends which nurseries they use. I got a broad opinion this way and successfully narrowed it down to a nearby nursery that was extremely popular.

The other upside of approaching it like this was that Jenny was enrolled in a nursery which some of her friends attended. From day one, she had some playmates that she knew and I had some mum contacts who could report back anything I needed to know. Strength in numbers definitely applied here.

So we found an extremely popular local nursery and managed to squeeze her in for a long midweek session. After a couple of 'settling in' sessions (all good nurseries will offer at least one), I could tell that she loved it. The relief was amazing.

Enjoying that free time

This meant I could spend my Wednesday afternoons doing all the not-so-important stuff that got put on hold for the rest of the week. I also got to enjoy some great quality time with Rosie and make up for the rest of the week when she got put to one side rather a lot. I started popping into town on these afternoons. Getting some shopping done was so much easier with just one baby on board.

If you can find a trustworthy nursery (and I would recommend asking as many mums as you can for their advice) it can really take the heat off you. On a Sunday evening, the impending week can be a little overwhelming if you don't have many plans and the weather's not being very nice.

Once your toddler is settled in they will come to love their nursery and look forward to their sessions.

Going back for more

If you already have a great nursery in place and you're struggling a bit, you can always increase your toddler's sessions for a few weeks while you regroup and your newborn gets a bit older.

Just knowing that nursery-based time is taken up with fun, creativity and friends can really take the pressure off you as primary entertainment-provider. If you know that your toddler has a fun-filled afternoon at nursery coming up on a Wednesday, you can get away with staying at home on Tuesday or Thursday without feeling guilty.

When Rosie got a little bit older, I decided to split Jenny's one long afternoon session and spread it over two afternoons. It was getting difficult picking her up during rush hour and Rosie would always seem to want a feed at the very point we were leaving.

Having two afternoons taken care of really helps. Although Jenny is spending pretty much the same amount of time at nursery, it seems to free up what feels like a lot more hours for getting stuff done.

The benefits of nursery

Joining the nursery has really improved Jenny's social skills. She adores playing with other children now, which in turn makes play dates more pleasant. I can highly recommend using a good nursery when you're dealing with a new baby.

If you're not comfortable with nurseries (everyone feels differently), you might consider using a childminder. They tend to be cheaper and most are registered with the appropriate authorities.

When you use a childminder, your toddler may well get more one-on-one attention in a calm, family environment. Many of them also organise fun expeditions which your toddler will love.

Or if you're lucky enough to have relatives nearby, you could try asking them to take your toddler for a regular slot each week. I have a friend whose sisters also have kids so they do a childcare swap between the three of them and it works really well.

It's easy to feel guilty when you're handing your child over to be looked after by someone else but as long as you've done your research and can trust these carers, your toddler will have a blast and return to you fresh and happy. It doesn't matter how much you love each other, a regular change of scene (and face) is always beneficial.

Baby and toddler-friendly outings

Tip for the day: Set up a travel cot in your living room so you have somewhere safe to put the baby while you answer the door/feed your toddler etc. You can also pop a baby gym in there so they can kick about safely while you and your toddler play.

Every Friday we go to a toddler group at a local church hall. I used to avoid toddler groups after being subjected to ones full of cliquey women who had no time for newcomers. My confidence as a mother wasn't great back then either so I didn't really enjoy them.

But one Friday morning about 6 months ago, I decided Jenny really needed to get out of the house so we braved a local group I'd discovered through web forums. Immediately I knew we'd stumbled upon something wonderful. Every group we had been to before had been a little uninviting but the mums here were warm and extremely welcoming. And there was a tonne of cake.

We soon found our place in the group and have been going ever since. We took a few weeks off just before and immediately after Rosie was born, but went back as soon as we were able. Loving arms were flung wide to cuddle Rosie while I enjoyed a cup of tea, put my feet up and enjoyed watching Jenny play. And she loved being able to climb into my unoccupied lap every now and again for a cuddle.

If you can find a group such as this that works for you, it'll be a godsend once you're juggling your two under two.

This is my number one baby and toddler-friendly outing.

Soft play areas

Number two on my personal list is soft play areas. If you can find one with a good-sized toddler area, you're on to a winner.

Jenny, Rosie and I often head there on rainy afternoons. Jenny goes mental and runs around for a couple of hours, Rosie sleeps/feeds/sleeps and I am able to keep an eye on Jenny while looking after her sister. It's also a great place to meet new friends, especially during quieter sessions.

It gets a little costly once your toddler heads towards three years old but for

£6 or thereabouts I can entertain Jenny for at least two hours. And that's money well spent in my book. Plus our local play area does a loyalty card which gives us a free visit about once a month.

Visiting friends

My number three baby and toddler outing is visiting a friend's house. Make that an understanding friend's house; it certainly helps if they have a toddler too. With luck, their kid(s) and yours will entertain one another while you and your friend enjoy cuddles with your newborn.

Bear in mind though that in this situation you're going to have to keep your finger on the button, discipline-wise. When playing with a friend of or near their own age, your toddler is likely to push the boundaries even more than at home. Especially if there are two adults present to show off to. So it may not be quite as relaxing as you first imagine, but it's a good learning environment if you stay on your game, and the adult company helps to keep you sane.

Play parks

Number four: enclosed play parks. Not too big or you'll end up leaving your newborn at one end while you chase your toddler to the other.

You may live in the safest area around but chances are you wouldn't be too thrilled with leaving your baby unattended. Providing your toddler is sure on their feet and aware of being careful, they can enjoy climbing, swinging and monkeying to their heart's content while you jiggle the double buggy nearby.

NB: If you have a slightly younger toddler who isn't yet walking confidently, this might not be quite such an enjoyable outing. But if your newborn is sleeping soundly in a baby carrier or settled nearby in the pram, you can still pop your older child in the baby swings and help them down little slides.

The zoo

Number five on my list is the zoo. We have a great one nearby and I challenge you to find a toddler who doesn't love animals. This is the perfect outing if you're blessed with good weather.

As with play park outings, you can wear your newborn and use a lightweight stroller for your toddler. Zoo entry can be a little costly but if you take plenty of supplies, you can easily kill a whole afternoon. If you're blessed with a toddler who will sleep in their stroller (unfortunately we are not) you could spend the whole day there.

A lot of zoos offer loyalty incentives for repeat visits.

Go for a walk

Number six: go for a good old-fashioned walk. Load up the double buggy (or whatever you use for transport) and push off for a stroll.

This is great exercise for you, your newborn will probably sleep and you'll almost definitely encounter a play park/enclosed area along the way for your toddler to have a run around. It's surprising how refreshing a stroll around your local park is and you'll develop killer toned arms from all that pushing.

If your toddler is old enough, you can play games such as 'I spy' as you go. And have a snack ready to keep them occupied if they start to get bored.

It's no lie that fresh air helps babies and toddlers to sleep better, so you'll be glad you made the effort.

Out and about with help

Finally anywhere you can go with friends/relatives is a great idea. Since having Jenny, I've found some lovely friends whose children are approximately the same age as her.

If we go out together, their toddler and mine can play happily together under the watch of a friend while I focus on Rosie. Or I can run around with them while my companion enjoys some cuddles with the baby.

Never underestimate how keen people are to cuddle cute little babies!

Bonding with your newborn

Tip for the day: If, like me, you're a fan of the swaddle, try looking up the 'double swaddle how to' video online. Even our little Houdinis couldn't get out of that one.

Recently, Graham and Jenny jetted up to Scotland to go to his grandmother's 90th birthday party. I drove them to the airport and seeing him carry her off into Departures with her little Winnie the Pooh backpack just about broke my heart.

Freedom!

But as I drove away, I felt so unencumbered. When Jenny arrived, I really struggled to look after her at times but now that I've grown accustomed to having two under two, just looking after one of them feels like a holiday.

Parenting is such a steep learning curve that what we struggle with at first, we quickly grow used to. It's yet another reason I don't think anyone should panic before welcoming another child.

Focusing on the little one

Being home alone with Rosie really highlighted just how little attention she gets on a day-to-day basis. I try to play with her as much as possible but more often than not, she just naps upstairs for most of the day, or wriggles on her play gym while I entertain Jenny.

I know this will change as she gets older and starts sleeping less, but it makes me feel incredibly guilty. And I do worry that I will look back on these early months and feel like I didn't try hard enough to bond with Rosie.

With all of that in mind, it's definitely worth organising some time each week to spend alone with your baby. It will help with any guilty feelings and you'll love having quality time with them.

Getting some help

If you aren't sending your toddler to nursery, try to make sure your partner/a friend/a family member can help you out by taking your toddler somewhere for a couple of hours once a week. The newborn weeks are so precious and you'll feel so much better if you make the most of them wherever possible.

In terms of things you can do with your newborn, I know I was at a loss with Jenny. I would sit on the sofa with my new baby, crinkling pasta bags in her face and waving wooden spoons around. She didn't really care! Really, all your newborn needs is you. You'll remember this from the early days with your first baby: just one silly face pulled over and over again will reward you with endless smiles and gurgles.

Here are some other lovely things you can do to bond with your baby while your toddler is otherwise occupied:

- Wear them everywhere! It's not always possible to have them close to you, especially when you're using a double buggy a lot. But while your toddler isn't around, use a sling or baby carrier to hold them close to you when you go out or do the housework.
- Have a bath together if they're big enough. It can be tricky but I found from 6 weeks I could comfortably have Rosie in with me in her little seat. Just make sure to use a non-slip mat in there and have everything ready for when you get out.
- Have them nap on you. It's a luxury you probably won't be able to afford while your toddler is around. So settle down with a good film and great snacks and have your baby fall asleep on your chest.
- Learn baby massage – there are videos online about how to do this and it's a great bonding exercise. You may be able to find a course locally if you can commit to it.
- Sing – even if you're tone deaf, your baby will love the sound of you singing softly to them.
- Get a stack of books and read them together lying down on your bed.
- Mimic the little sounds they are making. They'll feel like they're really communicating with you, it's very cute!

If you don't feel immediately bonded with your baby, don't panic. Think back to when your first baby was brand new. You might have fallen in love with them at first sight, but many parents don't immediately feel deep-rooted kinship with their newborns.

When you have two under two, it is easy to assume that a lack of immediate attachment is because you're so busy with the older sibling. But give it time and trust those instincts that you've picked up so far. They won't let you down.

Helping your children to bond with each other

Tip for the day: Keep a stash of nappies, wipes, clothes, towels, long life snacks, juice boxes and plastic bags in your car boot. An impromptu stop-off somewhere becomes so much easier if you've got back-up.

Bonding with your baby is probably at the top of your list of Most Important Things. But it was a few weeks before it really dawned on me: I had to make sure these new siblings bonded with each other too, as often as possible.

Siblings are the best

I have very strong friendships with each of my three sisters and I am really keen for my girls to grow up to be just as close. My earliest memories are of playing games (and fighting) with my sisters and we were each other's best friends from very early on.

I adore my sisters and they have been my saving grace on countless occasions; it's one of the main reasons I was so thrilled that my two under two are girls.

The siblings that play together...

When baby number two arrives, the first few weeks are just about getting your head around your new routine. But once things have settled somewhat and your newest baby starts to develop a bit of character, you can have all kinds of fun by using one to entertain the other (at the risk of making them sound like Punch and Judy puppets). Getting them to play together helps your toddler see the newcomer as a new friend rather than competition.

Anything you can do to help your toddler see your new baby as 'fun' will be a huge help. Jenny and I like to mimic Rosie's funny little baby noises and play games with her to make her smile or laugh. Jenny is so obviously chuffed to bits when something she's done makes her sister laugh.

Games they'll both love

Jenny loves it when Rosie plays 'Peekaboo' with her. Sometimes I'll hold Rosie in my arms and make her head appear around the doorframe while Jenny is eating her lunch. They both love it. And Jenny loves to tickle Rosie to try and get chuckles out of her. With all the 'this little piggy' and 'round and round the garden' action songs, you can quite easily while away a happy hour cuddled up on the sofa with your little ones.

Communication

Above all, I have found that talking helps ease any feelings of rivalry. Fortunately, Jenny's speech improved ten-fold after Rosie arrived and she was able to understand a lot more. Verbalising everything I'm doing when I'm busy with Rosie keeps Jenny involved and teaches her lots of new vocabulary. She likes to mimic me and add her own bits:

Me: "Mummy is getting Rosie's bottle ready"
Jenny: "Yes, Mummy is getting Rosie's bottle ready nice and warm"

You can also use words to get your toddler to explain what they are feeling. If they seem frustrated with the new baby, you can try to explain their feelings for them. So if they take a playful swipe at their sibling, instead of shouting and disciplining, you can explain that you understand why they did it (more often than not I think it's to see how the little one will react) but that it's not okay.

Try saying; "You tried to hit your brother/sister because you want to see what they will do. But it's not nice to hit so you mustn't do it again". It'll be much easier on both of you than shouting/overreacting.

Fond memories

When you're holding your baby, talk to your toddler. Explain how much you love the baby and how much you love them too. When Jenny's feeling a bit left out: she tugs at my leg and says 'Two babies!' to signal that she wants me to hold her too. She picked this up from me from the very first day in the hospital when I held them both and got a bit mushy. It's wonderful that she's after attention but doesn't want it at her sister's expense.

Try asking your toddler if they remember having cuddles with you when they were tiny - show them photos.

Snaphappy

And while we're on the subject of photos, get LOADS of your children together. You can get them printed and put them up all over the house. When your toddler is displaying a bit of jealousy, show them a picture of them cuddling the baby. It'll help reinforce that bond they feel with their baby brother or sister and you'll have some priceless shots to admire for years to come.

Making sure that your toddler still feels like they have some power in the house will help. The more you can convince your toddler to help out with the baby, the more grown up they will feel and, in turn, the more protective they will become of their sibling.

So make sure you talk to your toddler all the time, tell them you understand how they feel. Even if you feel a bit silly at first, it'll work wonders for relationships throughout the home.

Potty training

Tip for the day: If your toddler isn't a fan of having their teeth brushed (that'll be all toddlers then), get them to choose a song which you will sing for them while you brush. You must keep brushing until the song's finished - which is entirely under your control.

A few people suggested getting Jenny potty trained while I was pregnant to cut down on nappy changing time once the new baby arrived. But there was no way she was ready physically or emotionally and I'm no fan of wee-soaked upholstery.

There's always a full nappy

I must admit it was tricky keeping on top of the nappy changes and there were a few occasions where poor Jenny came to me with hers hanging around her knees. Fortunately there was no missing the number twos; those can be smelt from halfway up the M5.

Preparations

I have a causal aim to get Jenny using the potty by about two and a half. As a bit of prep, the other day I went shopping and bought a little blue potty, some stickers and a copy of 'I want my potty!' by Tony Ross (a great book for the cause).

Jenny and I spent a while decorating her new loo, writing her name on it with permanent marker and popping stickers all over it. I gave an animated performance of 'I want my potty!' several times and later on she wanted to read it to herself – while sitting on her throne.

A day later she came to me and said 'nappy off!' and went to watch some cartoons, bare-bottomed on her new favourite seat. Nothing has come out as yet but I think it's great that she's not scared of it.

This gentle introduction to potty training was stress-free and enjoyable. Although at the time of writing she's not yet using the potty, she's certainly not scared of it and I would even go so far as to say she kind of loves it.

Wait until you're all ready

It can be tempting to go in guns blazing when your baby arrives, but the stress it'll cause (not to mention the cleaning) is not worth it. Better to juggle two little ones in nappies for a few months and come to it when everything's fallen into place and your toddler seems totally up for it.

Here are some tips I've picked up so far:

- Take your toddler shopping for 'big girl/boy pants'. Make a big fuss.
- If they do their first wee/poo on the potty, call someone (even if you have to fake the conversation) to tell them excitedly. Make a big fuss.
- Block out a week to really tackle it, rather than stop/starting according to your busy schedule.
- Make up a 'potty song' to sing every time they take the throne. It can help keep them on there while things get moving.
- If they're at nursery, get the staff to comply with any techniques you've employed (including making a big fuss).
- If they have an accident, do NOT make a big fuss. Just say 'never mind!' and clean it up quickly without fanfare.
- Let them flush the loo when you tip their wees/poos away. They'll become comfortable with the noise for when they start using the big loo.
- Use treats if you're comfortable doing so. A chocolate button or two is a great incentive to get things moving.
- Put their teddies on the potty. Make a big fuss.
- Get some elasticated tracksuit bottoms. They're usually pretty cheap and are easy to pull up and pull down.
- Don't force it: if you ask if they need to go and they say 'no', wait a while before asking again. If they ask to go of their own accord, make a big fuss.

As you see, you'll spend an awful lot of time clapping your hands and cheering for bodily functions. But it'll pay off in the end.

Finances

Tip for the day: When you move your toddler into a big girl/boy bed, don't be afraid to leave a box of toys in their room. Yes, they might get up and play with them but it stops them emptying all the drawers! And it's good opportunity to teach them about when it's time to sleep and when it's time to play.

You may well think that having another child is going to cost a fortune, especially if you have a child of the opposite gender on board.

But it really doesn't have to: most of the equipment you'll have acquired with number one may well be gender-neutral - even if it's not, I don't imagine your brand new baby boy will whinge about looking stupid in a pink bouncy chair.

Ask around

You've probably collected a fair few mum friends by now who will heap clothes and other baby bits on you. If they haven't, try asking. I know even with our girls there are bags of stuff that we just don't use. But we keep hold of them in case others might like them.

A lot of the children's centres I have visited have notices up all over the place from people who are struggling to find what they need and would love to buy second hand.

Freecycle

I think Freecycle.org is one of the best websites ever built. If you haven't yet had a look, stop by.

It's proof that one man's trash really is another's treasure. I found a cot on there for my sister's baby, a stroller for us, a chest of drawers (in lovely pine) and a venetian blind amongst other things. And as the name suggests, it's all free.

Two things:

1. This isn't a hard and fast rule but if you are going to use Freecycle, try to put some stuff on there in return. You may have a pile of old books or videos that are gathering dust or even some stray rubble in your garden. The site relies on give as well as take, so do your bit if you can. It's great for de-

cluttering or getting rid of large items easily.

2. Be polite. I've put some great items up on Freecycle before and the people who email saying 'Yeah alright I'll take it' don't really do it for me. I always choose the nicest-sounding person who makes the effort to write a nice message.

Overall, we didn't have to buy anything apart from our double buggy (and that was £30 second hand – hardly used. We hit Gumtree for that). Nappies and formula are just about covered by the second lot of child benefit (about £14 per week for your second baby).

Nappies

When Jenny arrived I would only put her little bum in top-of-the-range nappies. But it wasn't long before I decided to experiment with the supermarket's own brand – and I haven't looked back. I'm not talking the really *really* cheap ones, they may be fine but I'm not up for experimenting. Mid-range nappies are absolutely fine and are a good few pounds cheaper than branded nappies.

Meal planning

My other main spending saviour was meal planning. If you can sort out your week's meals (and after a month you'll have a rotatable shopping list without things getting mundane) in advance, you'll spend a lot less on bits and pieces throughout the week. Get it delivered for the first few weeks as getting to the supermarket with your two in tow is not the easiest of tasks.

The weekly shop can be a big expenditure so if you're struggling with it, shopping online can help you bypass the temptations and make the most of any special offers. If you don't have one, it's worth investing in a freezer (or upgrading to a tall one if yours is a bit small). I occasionally head to the local shop near to closing time and buy up anything freezable that has been reduced. Meat, especially.

So don't panic: early on, finances are quite manageable. I qualified for government maternity allowance and also stockpiled some savings while I was working before Rosie arrived. With that and the fact that our mortgage isn't through the roof, we get by without having to give up too much.

Juggling your money can be exhausting and I'm rubbish at managing what's coming in and what's going out. But motherhood has forced me to be a little more responsible.

Bathing your two under two

Tip for the day: Invest in some bath crayons for your toddler. While you're trying to see to your baby, these will keep your eldest well entertained. Oh and buy some industrial strength cleaner to get the damn stuff off again.

Most of the time I try to bath Jenny while Rosie is asleep or vice versa. But sometimes we don't have the luxury of time.

So today I decided to tackle bathing them both together. I've done it before and it's been a total nightmare. They both seemed to want to get out at the same time, Rosie was terrified of the big bath and I'd forgotten to lay out everything I needed afterwards. Plus the bathroom was freezing.

Rosie's meltdowns are few and far between which makes it all the more painful to listen to her cry when she does. I realised that perhaps I needed to think through my approach in a lot more detail.

So I researched, had a good old think and then and tested a new technique earlier - with success!

My technique

- Make sure both children's towel, clothes and nappies are laid out beforehand, preferably on your large bed so you have somewhere soft to put them down.
- If it's a chilly day, put the heating on a good half hour before you begin. You can put your babies' towels on the radiators ready for when they get out.
- Set up some music. A laptop, phone or tablet can be placed nearby (though obviously well out of splashing range) to play your toddler's favourite singalong songs and buy you extra time.
- If feeding time is near, have a bottle ready for your newborn to comfort them when they get out. However, it's generally a good idea to make sure your baby's tummy is full when you bathe them.
- Put your toddler in the bath first and, if you have one, use the shower attachment to fill your baby bath on the floor beside the tub. Make sure you haven't forgotten to put the plug in (yes, this really happened).
- Remove anything that can scoop water up from your toddler's bath

unless you want a flooded floor while you bathe your newborn.

- Put your newborn into their bath next and involve your toddler with washing him/her by asking them to pass you sponges, baby wash etc. It's a very good idea to have a newborn bath seat. We have a wire outline with a towelling cover which is a godsend.
- Get your newborn out when clean, bundle them up and take them to be dried, clothed and fed as close to your toddler as possible, so you can keep an eye on them.
- Hopefully your newborn will be happy to be swaddled up and put into their cot/basket while you see to your toddler but if not, try popping them in a baby chair where they can watch you both. I usually put Rosie under her musical mobile. With all the doors open, I can see her from the bathroom.
- Let your toddler play for as long as you can or as long as they want to. Involve them in scrubbing themselves clean.
- Get your toddler out and get them dressed while telling stories, singing songs - whatever you can do to keep them from getting wriggly and stroppy.
- Leave both baths as they are – you can deal with emptying and cleaning them later.

As your baby gets older, you'll find bathtime is a great way to while away half an hour, so you'll quickly become an expert.

But don't feel like you have to bath them both every day. We manage it once every three days on average, unless one of them gets particularly messy.

Oh and an extra tip – get loads of toys and one of those nets that hold them all. They suction to the side of the bath. Your toddler will love pulling them out one by one and there'll be several in there that are good for your baby to gum on once they start sitting up in the bath.

Your social life

Tip for the day: If you're planning an outing, it's usually best to organise it for the afternoon. This gives you the morning to potter and play and ensures good naps before you embark on your adventure.

When Rosie was about two months old, my sister got married. The girls were bridesmaids, the rain held off and we all had an amazing day.

The wedding was well-timed for me. In the run-up, there were a few opportunities to go out and have a good time, something I didn't do enough of when Jenny was tiny. I felt it would be wrong to get dressed up, go out and party while she was at home, surely perishing…What kind of a mother goes out and has *fun*?

There are thousands of people out there ready to make new parents feel guilty for wanting to have a life outside of the home. Ignore them, and get your glad rags on.

The old days

Before I had children, my social life was almost unmanageable. I remember planning my weeks so that I would have a guaranteed night off to recover. And even then I'd probably have some spontaneous adventure on that night, too.

Socialising is a big part of me. It took a little while for us to pin it down but my husband and I realised that some of our stormiest periods were when I was staying in an awful lot, feeling chained to the house.

The promise of a good night out at the end of a difficult week is enough to save my sanity when things are getting a bit uncontrollable.

Have some fun!

So I've refused to guilt-trip myself about socialising since Rosie arrived. Once we stopped exclusively breastfeeding, I was able to enjoy a night out here and there (or even a night in with my sisters) and feel like myself again. Six evenings out of seven I'm at home so there's nothing to feel guilty about.

Of course, socialising isn't just about going out and having some drinks. It depends on your nature, but socialising is socialising, however you enjoy it.

And I really believe it's crucial when you're at home with your children all day.

Sports

I recently joined a netball team in a bid to shed those pesky remaining pregnancy pounds. I love netball and played a lot before I moved down to the south west. I've struggled to find a team since being here but a friend at toddler group decided to set one up. It's a guaranteed (healthy) evening out for me every week and the exercise is great for my general mood. I'm such a lazy person by nature but when I force myself to take on challenges like this, it always makes me feel great. And I'm a happier mum because of it.

Many of my friends took up running when they had their children. There is something really cathartic about pounding the pavements either first thing or at the end of a hard day.

Make sure you have some stuff going on so that you don't just feel like a parent, and nothing else. At first, you probably won't have the energy but it's very easy to get stuck in a rut of not really doing much once the kids are in bed.

When they're older, you may feel like getting a babysitter booked and going out for a meal with your partner. Make sure your time away from the house is a healthy balance. With friends, family and exercise, you'll have a much happier outlook.

Moving your toddler into a big bed

Tip for the day: Buying your toddler some fancy new bedding can help the transition to big bed go a little more smoothly. Get something featuring their favourite character if you can.

If I'd done my research, I would have transferred Jenny to a toddler bed a few months before Rosie arrived. After some belated reading, I discovered that the ideal time to get your toddler into a bed is about 8 weeks before the little one makes its appearance. This gives your firstborn time to adjust to their new bed before the newborn pinches their old cot.

Oh well.

Softly, softly

We took a slow and steady approach to moving Jenny into a bed. A few weeks ago I bought her a duvet and pillow set to put in her cot. With much fanfare, we unveiled this new bedding to her and she was very excited (though she wanted to keep her old blanket for the first couple of nights for comfort – we let her).

We then dropped the bars of her cot so that she could climb out if she wanted to. Fortunately, this held little appeal for her and she only tried it a few times.

We set up the toddler bed in her room and kept her in the cot for a few nights, chatting to her at bedtime about the impending move to her 'big girl bed'.

When the time came to move her, she was totally happy with it. She still asks after her cot but we explain that Rosie needs to sleep in it now because it's for smaller babies. Anything that makes her feel like a 'big girl' is very effective.

Moving your baby into their own room

A lot of people don't like to move their babies into their own room until 6 months – or even later if possible. It's all down to personal preference but we all started sleeping better when we moved Jenny to her own room at 12 weeks.

We will be moving Rosie at about 16 weeks. I love having her asleep next to me but every little snuffle and stretch wakes us up. When she was feeding several times a night, it made sense to have her right next to us but now we're down to just one or two feeds.

You will probably find that your baby settles themselves a lot better once they're in their own room. But everyone feels differently about when to do this. Trust your instincts.

Extra tips for moving from cot to toddler bed:

- The top tip is: be consistent - and it ties in with the next tip…
- Don't move them until you're absolutely sure they're ready. Once you make the move, you really must stick with it and don't backtrack by putting them back into their cot.
- Talk to your toddler - they understand a lot more than we realise sometimes so make sure you tell them lots about their new bed before the transition happens. You could make up bedtime stories about it or look for videos/stories about this big step.
- Use a side rail - if the bed doesn't come with one, I believe you can buy siderails to attach to the bed. Falling out can make the new bed seem far scarier to a toddler so preventing tumbles is a good idea. You can place pillows along the floor in case they do fall but they'll probably end up getting moved around by your toddler. Some people use a futon mattress.
- Keep your routine the same - whatever bedtime routine you were using before, stick to it. It's important to keep everything the same aside from the new bed so that it doesn't feel like a huge upheaval.
- Stay positive and always encourage your toddler. They are bound to resist their new bed so make sure you keep them interested by talking about what an exciting new step it is.

Toddler sleep problems

Tip for the day: Get photos printed! You may have had gazillions printed when your first came along but now there never seems to be enough time. But you'll regret if you don't. Nominate one evening to get them organised and another to put together a photo album for each of your babies. They'll treasure it for years to come and you can use the inside front page to record all their firsts.

You might find, as we did, that your toddler's sleep becomes more erratic the older they get. I'm assured that by the age of three or four, Jenny's sleep habits will become more predictable. God, I hope so.

Phases

Jenny has always gone through phases with her sleep, especially when she learned to crawl and then walk. She spent about 6 weeks just after her first birthday waking in the night and crying. She would then settle down for a few weeks and then it would begin again.

It seems that her most consistent sleeping problems started about 2 months before Rosie was due and continue to this day. Sleepless nights are manageable when you're just dealing with a newborn but when you're up all night with both children, being full of the joys of summer the next day is pretty much impossible.

Ups and downs

Right now, Jenny is perfectly capable of sleeping 6.30pm – 8am without any trouble. She's also capable of thundering around her room like a baby elephant for two hours in the middle of the night. This may or may not be after a two-hour standoff at bedtime and may or may not precede a 6.30am wake-up call.

After reading plenty of online resources (mostly posted by mothers going through the same thing), I'm reassured that this is perfectly normal. However, it's not always perfectly manageable so we have put some new measures in place that usually contribute to a more restful night.

1. We've shunted her daytime nap (which she definitely still needs) forward by an hour to around 1pm. If naps don't work out, we'll

just push through to bedtime. Late naps (after 3pm) make bedtime absolutely impossible.

2. Before bedtime, one of us will lie with her reading stories to her and generally calming her down ready for a restful night.
3. We make sure she gets plenty of fresh air and exercise – particularly in the afternoon.
4. If she does get up in the night/too early, we have a unified approach: no communication and gently depositing her back in bed. The frequency of these visits spreads out each time. The first few nights it needed to be done about 20 times (I lost count at about 15) but with perseverance it got better.

It doesn't always work but I would say it's crucial to make necessary changes if this starts happening to you. We went from having a toddler who could be doubled-up giggling one minute and fast asleep the next, to a much trickier. Things had to be re-evaluated, especially once we had two children to deal with.

More tips from tired parents

Other ideas that I picked up during my extensive research on this topic are outlined below. We've tried them all: some worked, some didn't and some don't really apply but I thought my research shouldn't go to waste:

- If bath time calms your toddler down, use it nightly until sleep improves. Try using one of those bubble baths that promote sleep.
- Make sure you have a bedtime routine in place that lasts at least half an hour. This can be all or some of the following: bath, bottle, pyjamas, story time, singing, relaxation music and cuddles.
- No TV an hour before bed as it can over-stimulate some children.
- If your toddler is hopeless at falling asleep without you, take a book in to read while they drift off. Sit with your back to them and avoid any interaction. It'll keep your mind off that cool glass of wine waiting for you downstairs and make the whole process go a lot faster.
- If your toddler is a bit anxious, tell him/her you'll come back to check on them in a few minutes. Do so (but wait as long as you can) and you may well find they've drifted off anyway.
- If your little one does get up and come to you in the middle of the night, you could let them get into bed with you. However, this might

create a more long-term problem. If you value your bed space, you're better off being firm and putting them back to bed each time. It might take an endless amount of time at first but over a few nights, they'll get the picture.

- If your toddler is old enough and good with numbers, buy a digital clock for their room. You can tell them not to get up before the first number is seven or eight. If your toddler can't quite grasp it, try putting a sticker over the minutes and just unveiling the hour, so they only need to cope with one set of numbers.
- If you have an early waker but a good sleeper in general, some parents report success by gently rousing them (so they wake slightly but settle again) about an hour before they normally wake. Yes, this may involve you getting up at 4am but if done consistently over a few days, most people report an improvement in their morning alarm call.

Trying to look after a toddler and a newborn on very little sleep is one of the hardest things I've ever had to do. But it's definitely got so much easier given time, hang in there!

When you can't get out of the house

Tip for the day: Put your toddler to work! Teaching them about tidying up after themselves from a young age will pay off in the future. Show them how to put their toys away, make up a song about it, wear a stupid hat. Anything to make it fun. And before long you'll have a proper little helper.

Even with the best intentions, some days it just seems impossible to get out of the house with two children under two. Whether it's illness, bad weather or finances that are keeping you locked up indoors, it can be very difficult to keep your toddler entertained.

On the plus side, on cooped-up days, both children are likely to take good quality naps, which in turn should provide you with an easier time at night.

Outside

We are extremely fortunate to have a garden which is just about big enough for Jenny to while away an hour or two playing on her slide, shooting next door's cat with her water pistol or poking insects with sticks.

Earlier today I heard her crying 'I don't want it!' from the garden. I looked out to see her frantically shaking her hand trying to dislodge the slug that was clinging to her index finger.

Keeping watch

Our kitchen overlooks the garden and we have French windows so I can potter about with the laundry or washing up while I watch her play. Or I can just get stuck in kicking balls about with her all the while being close enough to the house to hear Rosie on the monitor. Having a good view of your garden is crucial for avoiding accidents.

Let's bounce!

Recently we took delivery of a 10-foot trampoline complete with enclosure which has taken up permanent residence in the garden. Jenny's favourite thing in the world is bouncing; it's no coincidence that her first word was 'Tigger'.

I ummed and ahhed for weeks about whether it was worth the investment but I have it on good authority that this blessed piece of equipment will entertain our little ones for years to come. Plus anything that gets them outside and exercising is good in my book.

Jenny adores it, and so do any friends who come to visit, not all of them children.

Inside

If you don't have a garden, you will have to get creative indoors. Messy play is always a great way to spend a couple of hours of your long afternoon. Personally, I'm not a huge fan of the messiness in general but I'm getting to grips with it.

I saw a great idea online recently: get some sealable, transparent bags and squirt some paint/coloured water into them. Seal them up (tightly!) and tape them to a window. Your toddler will love squishing the colours around and mixing them into each other – and you won't have a ruddy great mess to contend with afterwards.

Then there are jigsaws, building blocks, drawing (Jenny's favourite), painting and learning numbers/letters/colours. The web is a great resource for learning tools such as songs and basic games for toddlers. Most of these activities can be done while your newborn naps, kicks about on a play gym, or cuddles up to you in a sling or baby carrier.

You get out what you put in

I used to be guilty of being a bit lazy when it came to entertaining Jenny but I've had to pull my finger out and make life a bit more interesting for her – or else she makes life pretty difficult for me. She's really enjoying learning new things and it's a joy to watch.

It's made parenting her even more rewarding. When she starts singing the 'abc' song or counting for me while I scoop out Rosie's formula, it's wonderful to know that it's mostly down to the work I've put in. I hope I have the time to provide the same for Rosie.

Ditching the dummies

Tip for the day: If you don't have one already, get your toddler a little toy pram/buggy. Jenny has one and she brings her doll along on shopping trips. You can push your babies along together, they love it!

We love dummies. In honesty, we would probably be divorced now had it not been for dummies. From day one, both of our babies had to suck. Which I, as a breastfeeder, was naturally thrilled with. The only thing we could pacify either of them with was a breast or a finger.

When it got to the point where I was in severe pain and we felt icky putting potentially germy fingers in their gobs (they never felt clean enough no matter how much we scrubbed), we decided to invest in dummies. And life changed pretty much instantly.

Ups'n'downs

Yes there are downsides: they fall out, they need to be put back in again; they get dropped in the street, they must be cleaned (most of the time - come on, we've all done it). But I happily coexist with these problems for the relief dummies bring when either baby is screaming in the back of the car or just won't go to sleep.

Dummy dependent

The problem now of course is that Jenny is two years old and still very much attached to her dummies. We haven't introduced the dummy fairy yet but that is my plan.

I've started by telling her daily that 'dummies are for babies and you're a big girl!'. She has started pulling her dummies out after naptime and telling me proudly "I not a baby, I big girl". She also sees Rosie with her dummies which only reinforces the point that she's outgrowing them.

When to do it?

If I was a tad stronger I'd get her to ditch the dummies now but frankly, I'm not in the habit of making life more difficult for myself. With the bed switching and Rosie's arrival, I think it's only fair to give her a bit more time, what's the harm?

So instead of being able to regale you with my experience, I'll share some tips I've picked up from friends and the web on how to get it right.

1. (and this is at the top for a reason) DON'T GIVE UP! Even if you have a few nights of total meltdown, you have to persevere once you get going.
2. Wean dummy use down to just nap/bed time for a few months before you get rid of them altogether. Again, be consistent.
3. As with potty training, try another Tony Ross classic: 'I want my dummy!' Reading this to your toddler should make the transition that bit easier. There are plenty of helpful books out there.
4. One friend used a mug tree to hang all her son's dummies off one night with the promise that each branch would hold a gift in replacement come morning. This was extremely successful as her little boy got involved with decorating the tree with stickers and crayons before bed. A lot of work for his mum though.
5. Autonomy really helps with transitional stuff so get them to choose – gifts, decoration, even a little card for the Dummy Fairy. It'll help them feel in control.

I am certain we'll have a few days/weeks of hell when we get rid of Jenny's dummies. It'll also be very difficult because Rosie will still have hers. But we just have to remember who's the boss – and stick to those guns! They won't be going off to university with a 'dumdum' so it has to happen some time.

Your love life

Tip for the day: Laugh! Monkeying around with your toddler and making them giggle can turn a really, really rubbish day into a much better one immediately. We all know the tricks to make our toddlers chuckle, even in their stinkiest of moods. Jenny and I do daft ballroom dancing. So if you've been a bit grumpy, paid a bit too much attention to the baby, or are just feeling a bit flat, get some giggles going. It really is the best medicine.

Any relationship that welcomes a child into it is bound to suffer a little bit. Our relationship was very new (**very** new) when we discovered I was pregnant. The pregnancy was planned, but just came along a lot faster than we thought it would. We were very lucky but very surprised!

So we had to work really hard to keep our relationship a happy one, especially as we were really still getting to know each other.

Making the time

When Jenny arrived, we struggled to make the time to just be a couple. This wasn't so much because of lack of time, I think it was lack of inclination. We still loved each other but tiredness and emotional hard work took its toll and I think both of us just wanted to be alone and chill out in our down time.

We had to remind ourselves to take the time to remember why we fell in love and spend a bit of quality time together, even if we didn't really feel up to it. Sticking a film on and cosying up on the sofa is a great way to be together without it requiring much energy.

Making a delicious dinner to enjoy together is another lovely way to add some freshness to things. It might feel a little forced at first, but don't let that put you off. I think that's why so many couples with babies struggle: they just feel that there's not much place for romance any more. But for the sake of your children and your happiness, it's vital.

Second time around

This time around, the same problems arose but at 4 weeks, we made sure we got Rosie into a good routine of going to bed around 7pm every night. We didn't do this until about 12 weeks with Jenny and we realised how much we'd missed having our evenings. Of course she was a fractious baby and she cried non-stop from 5-7 most night, which didn't help.

Fortunately, Rosie has settled into this routine well and it means that, with a bit of teamwork, we can sit down to a meal together most evenings. And there's still plenty of evening left for quality time - or an early night.

Getting out together

Last night we went out for dinner thanks to my eldest sister offering her babysitting services. It was so much fun to enjoy a glass of wine and some great food together without the distraction of a buzzing monitor, the television or a mound of washing up.

Rather than talking about the kids, moving house or any other day-to-day logistical complications, we just chatted. It was lovely learning new things about each other and just being a bit silly after too much wine.

Communicate

A lot of problems that arise between new parents are largely down to poor communication. Learning to talk about everything honestly and openly is difficult for some people. It certainly was for us.

But be as direct as possible about how you're feeling. Even if it makes you feel a bit silly, if it's bothering you, it must be important. If you don't generally communicate well as a couple, lay down some ground rules before you talk. Promise not to judge each other and just to listen. It's important that you both feel safe in confessing your troubles.

If you feel like there's a big imbalance when it comes to looking after the children, this is a crucial thing to talk about. It may be that your partner wants to do more, but doesn't want to interfere. Or perhaps you feel that they don't trust you to take full control when it comes to the children.

Problems such as these can really make a relationship rot. For your family's sake, and to protect your future, make sure you keep the lines of communication wide open.

Protecting your relationship

So try to make time for each other as often as you can. Go out/stay in for a nice dinner, share a bottle of wine and just talk, talk, talk.

It may feel like you have nothing left to give at the end of a hectic day, but just making sure you spend some decent time together at least once a week really does bolster your relationship and give it the best chance of surviving the challenges of having babies.

Enlist the help of family or friends to look after the children. Or look into hiring a trustworthy babysitter. You'll love getting to know each other as people again, rather than just as parents.

Two lots of teething!

Tip for the day: Get one of those bouncing stations for your baby (where they sit in a material sling surrounded by toys and bounce themselves up and down). I didn't bother the first time around but this time it's been a lifesaver. Rosie loves it, it knackers her out and it's really helped with her leg strength. The interactivity, songs and noises keep her really happy. We got ours second hand as it's a bit pricey for a new one.

I have a sneaking suspicion that Jenny is cutting the last of her molars. It came as quite a shock to me when a quick web search revealed that, crammed as her little mouth was, she was still missing two back molars on the top and two on the bottom.

Dealing with teething behaviour

Her behaviour recently has been challenging to say the least. Which, when dealing with a baby at the same time, is not anyone's idea of fun.

Sometimes it seems like everything is a battle and she has to get her way or we'll be in Tantrum Central. After a few days/weeks* of trial and error, I realised that the best way to handle my little diva is to offer her plenty of choice wherever possible.

* okay *months*

So if we're about to sit down to lunch, I ask if she would like pasta or sandwiches. Would she like it on a plate or in a bowl? And would she like to use her pink cup or the yellow? And would she rather Mummy bashed her head against the wall or the door?

Mind games

Making her feel like she is in control and is getting her way seems to limit the number of screaming fits. I make sure I offer choices only when her choice makes no odds to me. But she doesn't know that.

Most toddlers are fond of the word 'no' and my little darling is no exception. It can be hard to stay calm when she's being deliberately contrary but on the occasions that I do get frustrated, it makes things much worse and doesn't do my parenting any favours.

For example, when she shouts 'no Rosie!' right in her little sister's face and makes her cry, I do find it hard to stay collected. But if I shout back at her, I really don't have much of a leg to stand on.

Teething has raised the frequency of the 'no's to new heights; I'm not one to wish away my life but I'm looking forward to teething being a dim and distant memory.

Teething tricks

Going through this again after many months' freedom from the teething beast has reminded me what a struggle it can be. Rosie has just got her bottom two teeth and it's definitely had an impact on her normally sunny personality. And her nappies.

We've found that frozen chunks of banana saved our sanity on many occasions with our girls. That and teething liquids and powders (not the gel, they both just swallow that before I can get a decent amount rubbed in) which you may have to ask for at the pharmacy. They're not always put on display with the gels.

There was a brief period where the powders weren't on sale, allegedly because some cheeky little imps were using it to cut cocaine (how delightful). But they seem to be available again, thankfully.

Here are some other teething tricks I've gathered along my way:

- I've never got hold of one but many women swear by amber teething necklaces - a lot of them look pretty stunning as an added bonus!
- Wet a clean flannel and pop it in the freezer for half an hour. Your baby will love chewing on the ice-cold cloth. Add some juice if you want to make the whole experience even better for them.
- Similarly, you can freeze little fingers of bread for them to chomp on.
- Don't be afraid to use medicine if the poor thing is really suffering. Some bouts of teething are truly horrendous, so use infant paracetamol/ibuprofen if you think they need it, that's what it's there for.
- Try massaging your baby's gums. Give your hands a good scrub

and use your fingers to gently rub any areas that look red or inflamed.

Perspective

Teething's a very testing time and sometimes you wonder how you'll cope, but the truth is that the whole thing is very quickly forgotten once it's over. So try to keep some perspective and remember that the sunny little character you're more used to will return. Eventually.

I've known friends who have been driven to distraction by sudden dreadful behaviour, only to spot a new, white tombstone pop up days later. Then they say 'ohhhh...!' and feel rubbish and horribly guilty for the rest of eternity.

So if your toddler is being unusually naughty or having a lot of tantrums, take a deep breath and remember it'll be over soon.

Losing it

Tip for the day: If you're having a long day and are running out of ways to keep your little ones occupied, a bath is a good way to kill half an hour. Lots of toys + lots of bubbles = lots of fun. Why not get in with your toddler if your baby is napping?

I had the mother (pardon the pun) of all meltdowns last night. They do happen, no matter how many children you have. The all-encompassing emotional, psychological and physical nature of bringing up babies is bound to have some kind of impact occasionally.

A Very Hard Day

We'd all had a particularly rubbish night's sleep and Jenny had been hard work all day long (yep, teething). She seemed hell bent on pushing all my buttons and I was too tired to deal with it well. Throw into the mix a catalogue of other minor problems and we were on a collision course with some epic fallouts.

Jenny shouts, I shout, she cries, I feel guilty. She gets put to bed, she empties all her drawers. She gets up, she throws her lunch at me.

It's a cycle you'll be familiar with. It can be almost impossible to cope with a stroppy toddler while you're feeling really quite stroppy yourself.

Imbalance

While all of this is going on, dear little Rosie is getting ignored, which generates a freshly-baked batch of guilt. It's at these moments that my love for them coupled with my frustration tears at my heart in ways that I can't always cope with.

On our best days as parents, we might think we've cracked discipline and marvel at the little angel cavorting happily around the local park.

But then tiredness hits and it all goes to pot.

Use people!

On days like these, it's so important to lean on your support network.

If you have a supportive partner, use them. If family are offering help, accept it. I'm awful at the latter but I've learned that people genuinely mean it if they offer to shoulder some of my load for a few hours.

Being honest about the fact that you are struggling doesn't make you weak; it takes some guts to admit when you have taken on a bit too much and you can't quite cope. No one is going to berate you for it; they're far more likely to be annoyed at you for not using the help they've offered.

My support

I'm extremely lucky to have a calm, sympathetic husband who will comfort me even when I'm being a rotten witch, as I was last night. And as for my family, well you couldn't wish for a better bunch on your side.

This has been a tough chapter to write as I think we all have the same problem: we want to present a cool, collected front even if we're stewing on the inside. We want to appear as model parents at all times. We also don't want to seem unappreciative - having children is a blessing.

But admitting that you don't get it right all the time can be pretty liberating. Especially if you have someone to talk to who will tell you what a great job you're doing when you need to hear it most.

Time for you

Tip for the day: Do you own Jenga? The bricks are great for all sorts of games with your toddler, and your baby will love gumming on the smooth wooden bricks when they're teething (obviously supervise this closely!). Your baby can sit in their little seat and chew their bricks while your toddler builds towers, tracks, houses etc. A good early lesson in sharing.

If there's one thing that should be mastered early on, it's how to make sure you have a bit of time for yourself every single day.

Yes – every single day.

Chill out

It could be a hot bath in the evening while your toddler is sleeping and your partner feeds your newborn. It could be reading a few chapters of a good book while both babies are napping.

Or, if you're like me, it could be furiously (and therapeutically) scribbling down your thoughts for ten minutes whenever both children are asleep. Then editing out the naughty words.

Get out and about

It's also crucial to get out of the house occasionally. Last weekend, I left the children with Graham and took myself off to a local literary festival for a few hours. I watched some authors speak about their work. I wandered around the beautiful grounds and had a delicious lunch in the sun. All free from gallivanting children, dirty nappies and endless piles of washing up.

When I came home I felt completely rejuvenated, inspired and above all, happy as a clam. I immediately wrote three chapters of this book.

If there's something you're passionate about or even just mildly interested in, use your 'you time' to find out more about it. You never know what might turn into a hobby or even a new business venture.

Asking for help

As I've mentioned, I sometimes struggle to ask when I really need help. But since Rosie came along, I've had to knock that on the head.

When my husband comes through the door at the end of the day, I don't feel guilty for handing one of the children straight over to him for some help. After all, he is away from them all day which means a) he has probably missed them and b) he has a fresh attitude to dealing with their needs.

Make sure you ask your partner to help you. They may be tripping blissfully through life thinking you've got it all covered. And they're not mind-readers, so make sure they know what you need from them in order to stay sane.

Keeping each other happy

Your partner may work all the hours under the sun but their home life is not an extension of work. It's life and you both need to remember that your life together is about helping each other out as much as possible.

When Graham steps in and gives me some time to myself, he gets to spend some time with his girls and also gets the benefit of a much happier wife. So there's definitely something in it for him too.

In turn, if we've got a free afternoon, I'm much more inclined to send him off for some time to himself if I'm happy, relaxed and not feeling put upon.

The cyclical nature of helping and being nice to each other makes life a damn sight easier than muttering angrily behind each other's backs, snapping at each other for getting something wrong and generally feeling like you're in a badly-scripted episode of the Chuckle Brothers.

Why it's worth it

Tip for the day: If you don't have a slow cooker, get one! It'll be your best friend. You can gather ingredients and chuck them all in first thing and by dinner time you've got a meal ready to go. It'll also be well-cooked so you can puree some up if you're weaning.

If you're anything like me (and a very good friend of mine in the same boat), there will be the occasional day when you think 'Good God, why did I do this?'.

The upsides

When you feel this way, it can be helpful to stay positive and think of all the benefits.

For a start, you're getting those early years done in one fell swoop. Ever been to the park and seen older siblings playing happily while mum reads a book? That'll be us before we know it. Those who space their children farther apart have the same number of early years but they can easily span almost a decade.

Stuff. EVERYWHERE.

Sometimes it can seem like your house is crammed to the rafters with bags of clothes, old and new, cots, bouncers, car seats, highchairs and so on. But it'll only be this way for a couple of years.

Once both children are old enough, all the stuff that comes with them gets fewer and toys can be stashed in their rooms meaning you get some semblance of order back to the rest of your home.

You can also get out of the house or visit friends for the afternoon without having to pack three bags' worth of stuff.

School

When it comes to education, your children will be attending the same school together for a number of years. Think how much easier this makes the school run overall. There will be times that you'll need to make two trips, but it won't be long before your youngest moves up to join your eldest.

BFFs

And to my favourite reason: I am aware things don't always go this way but I'll be doing everything in my power to make sure these girls grow up to be the best of friends.

My sisters and I fought like cats and dogs so I know it won't always be easy, but now we couldn't be closer. I want that for my babies and I think having them grow up so close in age is one of the best ways to establish a close bond. They're more likely to be interested in the same things and therefore will play together more, learning that they can have acres of fun together.

I saw a photo on Facebook today: a friend of mine has two girls, now aged 4 and 5. They were cuddling each other grinning from ear to ear in gorgeous summer outfits. The comment below explained that they were off to the beach with friends and family.

I can mentally superimpose my girls' faces onto that picture and that's the image I keep in my mind. It reminds me why all of this is more than worth it.

Finding allies

Tip for the day: Bit gross this one but let your toddler have a good look at your baby's pooey nappies. When it comes to potty training, toddlers can get freaked out by their own poo (they don't generally see it before it's whisked away) so familiarising them with it will help in the long term.

My best friend is a fellow 'baby buncher' – more from her in the interviews section.

Her son (my godson) was just 9 months old when his sister was conceived. I find it tremendously helpful having her on hand for when things get a little bit challenging and we generally speak several times a week. Unfortunately we now live 300 miles apart but our support for each other has never wavered.

Well prepared

She is ahead of me in the game having had her second baby in 2010. As you know (you've bought this book after all), it's very useful having some forewarning of difficulties that might arise in the future. But mainly it's just priceless having someone to talk to who knows exactly how you're feeling.

I also have a couple of friends nearby who I've met since having my second baby. They are also parents of at least two very young children so they know exactly what life is like for me. I met two of them through toddler groups and another is an old friend from way back, with whom I never had anything in common until now!

Find some back-up

Finding allies is such a good idea. If you don't know anyone locally in your situation, try forums, social networks, playgrounds or baby groups to track some down. Their situation doesn't have to perfectly mirror yours, but people with more than one young child can be powerful supporters.

Try getting along to any rhymetime sessions, music groups or gym classes. These are popular boltholes for those juggling two or more young children and you'll soon find yourself striking up conversations. If you're too shy to approach new people, try asking existing friends if they know anyone with two under two.

Toddler groups are a lifesaver for meeting new people. Try going along to several, and stick with it. You won't be the newbie for very long. Most of these groups are very supportive places and you'll be especially popular if you arrive with a brand new baby, trust me!

Being there for each other

Building this support network will help you on your way to a successful time with your little ones. Heading out together will only reassure you that the difficulties you face are not yours alone. And occasionally, when the little ones have gone to sleep, you can both head out for a well-earned night off.

Non-mum friends

Although I think it's great to have friends who know your situation well, it's also vital to have some who don't.

When I got pregnant, I worried that I would lose touch with a lot of my non-parent friends, but they've all been extremely supportive. And I love getting together with them to talk about anything and everything – other than babies. I could bang on about my children for hours, but sometimes it's nice to talk about other things. Mum friends are fab, but you do often end up returning to one subject.

It's really easy to lose touch with friends who don't have children but try to make the effort. They can provide some much-needed sanctuary from the world of nappies and wipes when you need it most.

One under two

Tip for the day: If your baby is going through a catnapping phase, try waiting until they've been asleep for between twenty minutes and half an hour, then gently rousing them (not completely waking them, just so that their eyes flicker open then quickly close again). It worked for us and Rosie would sleep for at least another hour.

I've reached the point where I can no longer say I have two children under the age of two!

Jenny's second birthday has come and gone. It felt really special celebrating her first birthday as a big sister. With plenty of friends, food, fun and fizz, we had an amazing day.

It really feels like something of a milestone to me. Rosie is almost 15 weeks old and I have to say, things are definitely a lot easier now.

Rosie's routine is almost completely predictable (teething and illness aside), Jenny loves her to bits and probably can't remember life without her. And, mercifully, Rosie is only waking up for one feed at night. Jenny seems to have all of her teeth so is being a little angel – most of the time.

We're ticking along nicely and we have a family rhythm that works for us. It's taken some trial and error but we got there.

We've also made the (difficult) decision that we won't have any more children. Our little family unit is just what we've both always wanted and we are happy for it to stay this way.

All of this means we have a much merrier and more settled household than three months ago.

From what I had been told, I expected life to be in complete disarray for a lot longer than this. Probably about eighteen years.

The myth

This is the problem with other people. Not all of them, just a lot of them.

By now, you'll have had the same deluge of sympathetic looks and stupid comments that I had to put up with.

People love to make you feel like you are in for a dreadful time. They like to tell you that they almost had a breakdown when they had two under two, that they remember never sleeping, rarely eating and always arguing.

Or, worse, they don't have children and they look at you like you've taken a bullet in the arm and then requested another in the face.

You and them

But that's them, it's not you. And a lot of it is recalled with not-so-rose-tinted glasses or a complete lack of knowledge or experience. There are so many adages that are trotted out (think back to your first pregnancy – how many people started sentences with 'Just you wait..'?) when someone is pregnant.

The truth is, having two children under two is incredible and you'll never once regret having had your babies so close together.

You aren't stupid; you know it's not always going to be easy. But as we all know, anything worth having comes with its challenges.

Of course there will be times when you struggle. But there will be plenty more when your heart feels like it's going to burst with love. Like when you see your children holding hands, or your toddler wants to read a story to their little brother or sister, or fleeting moments when they're both asleep and looking utterly angelic.

It's a wonderful thing to witness your two children becoming the best of friends and your time, commitment and positivity will pay enormous dividends in the future. Have faith in yourself and your parenting skills and you won't go wrong.

Congratulations on your growing family!

Interviews

To contrast my experiences, I decided to interview some other parents about theirs. I am so grateful to all of them for their contributions.

Chrissy

Let me introduce you to my best friend, Chrissy. We met when I was about 18 years old and although we now live pretty far apart, we are still as close as always.

Chrissy's eldest is my godson. His arrival made me realise I was ready for babies of my own.

How old was your toddler when your second baby was born?

Lewis was 18 months when Isabella was born.

How old are your children now?

Lewis is now 3.5 and Bella has just turned 2.

What was your second pregnancy like?

After a brief spell of antenatal depression it was a breeze. The second pregnancy seemed to fly past as my focus was on Lewis. I wanted to get in as much quality time with him before I had to share my time.

I felt a little guilty towards the baby as I spent so much time daydreaming about my first child and researching each stage of the foetal development with my first pregnancy. And I just couldn't do that with my second.

The last few weeks were difficult. I found I didn't have the energy needed to run around after a toddler, and sitting down on the floor to play was hard on the hips.

I really enjoyed sharing moments with Lewis and the bump - he would wash my tummy in the bath and cuddle it.

What was your biggest fear about having two under two? And how did you cope with the reality?

When Bella was born Lewis was still very dependent on me, being only 18 months old. So my main fear was being able to cope with the demands of a newborn and the demands of a young toddler. I was concerned that I wouldn't be able to give Lewis the quality time he needed because I was dealing with a baby.

Reality was tough as there were plenty of times when one needed me whilst I was dealing with the other, so there was a lot of tears and guilt. I admit that I struggled my way through those first few weeks but it did get easier. Thankfully Bella was an easy, contented baby and I learnt to do a lot of things one-handed.

It sounds silly now but I do remember worrying that I loved my first child so much with all my heart, would I have enough love to give a second child? But as soon as I laid eyes on my daughter my heart doubled in size along with the love I had to give.

Tell us about your first day coping on your own with two under two.

My first day coping with them both was the day after Bella was born as my husband had to go into work.

It was really tough. All I wanted to do was cuddle my baby but I knew Lewis needed me too. So I had to discipline myself and put her down to sleep in her carrycot while I played with Lewis and gave him some quality time.

I remember realising pretty quickly that I couldn't leave them together for a second, so I erected the travel cot in the lounge and placed the carrycot inside so Bella would be safe from curious toddler fingers.

I do also remember it being a wonderful feeling though that Bella was finally here, sleeping next to us in her crib while I played with her big brother.

What is the best thing about having two under two?

Watching them playing and laughing together now, the age gap seems smaller. They are each other's best friend and they have a wonderful, strong relationship.

What's your top tip for coping with a baby and a toddler?

My top tip would be to get out to as many toddler groups as you can. There's always something to keep your toddler engaged while you cuddle your newborn. And there are plenty of people willing to cuddle your baby while you help your toddler with an activity.

The tea and biscuits help too.

Which product(s) made life easier for you?

I guess formula milk was the product that made life easier for me. Bella was breastfed but her last bottle at night was a formula bottle (given to her by my husband) at around 10.30pm.

This meant I could get my head down early and give myself a few uninterrupted hours sleep, which helped me deal with the following day better.

If you could go back to those early days and tell yourself one thing, what would it be?

I would tell myself to stress less about the behaviour of my first child. It took a turn for the worse and he started lashing out at me and Bella a few weeks after she was born. It was just a phase and a reaction to the new situation. But it corrected itself as we all settled into our new lives.

I regret not having a little more patience – hindsight is a wonderful thing!

How do you stay sane?

Wine and top friends who offer unlimited support. And the knowledge that these are precious years which need to be enjoyed. They grow up so fast.

Lewis

Lewis is a blogger (www.first-time-daddy.blogspot.co.uk), father to one boy and on the brink of welcoming another; at the time of interviewing, Lewis's wife was 36 weeks pregnant. He's kindly offered to share how many dads might be feeling in the run up to baby number two's arrival.

How many months will there be between your baby and toddler?

There will be around 17 months between Benjamin (born July 2011) and baby no 2 (Due end of December).

We really didn't plan it this way. We always planned on having a second but also planned to wait a while.

Hopefully when Benjamin was going to nursery, we could plan No2, but life has a funny way of throwing things at you and you have to deal with it. Now that baby No.2 is a reality, it might just work out for the best.

What's been the hardest part of the preparations for baby number two?

For me personally, the preparations haven't been too difficult.

Mostly it's a mental thing. Simply trying to imagine having 2 young children to look after blows my mind, and I'm not even the one doing most of the caring!

We are pretty well prepared. Due to the small gap between our two children, we already have most of the clothes, toys and furniture we need.

How have you helped your wife out during this pregnancy?

Like the first pregnancy, I have just tried to be as supportive as I can.

I try to make sure the house is as tidy as it can be with a toddler running around.

I try to make sure that anything that could place a strain on her and the baby is done by me, like lifting or moving anything. Unfortunately my wife doesn't always listen and starts lifting and moving things. She won't be told!

What are you looking forward to most about having two under two?

I'm looking forward to the bonding. I was the baby of the family with around

7 years between myself and my sister and around 10 years between me and my brother. Due to this I didn't really have anybody to play with.

Both my brother and sister, as you can imagine, were more concerned with other things going on in life. So I look forward to watching them play, laugh and learn together.

I have friends who also have children born close together. They're always telling me about all the fun times they have as a family and how it's nice for both children to always have someone to play with. They also tell me how often they fight with each other too, but we will cross that bridge when we come to it.

... and what are you most nervous about?

Far too many things!

Money: I always worry about money. I worry that we don't have enough to eat, pay bills, enjoy life. Needless to say I worry even more now we will have two mouths to feed. Which is why it's probably a good reason I don't look after the household finances. My wonderful wife is our bank manager and if she says we can afford something, then I trust that we can.

Time for Benjamin: I am conscious that when baby number two comes along, we must make sure we have time for our first child. I never want him to feel like he is second best.

Time for each other: we made a promise to ourselves that when Benjamin came along, we would still try to enjoy time as a couple. Go out, see a film, have a meal etc. If anyone offers to babysit, we made sure to take them up on it. We haven't done too badly up until now, but having two little ones will make it tougher.

Pressure on my wife: I've talked on my blog about how much I love my wife and what an amazing mum she has been to our little boy, but I worry that sometimes she puts too much pressure on herself. It's my job to make sure she doesn't but I worry I don't do that well enough!

What advice would you give to dads who have just found out baby number two is on the way?

Enjoy number one. Enjoy the quiet times when your first baby has gone to bed. Enjoy each other. Do anything your wife asks you to do – preferably the first time you're asked.

The best piece of advice I was given by a friend before becoming a dad was 'Just Do It'.

Baby needs changing? JDI! Ironing needs doing? JDI! Bathroom ceiling needs painting? JDI! (but don't get white paint on black tiles…)

How have you prepared your toddler for the baby's arrival?

We haven't really done anything differently so far. We don't want to break Benjamin's routine if we can help it.

He knows there is a baby in mummy's tummy. He gives mummy's tummy hugs and kisses and has, on the odd occasion, tried to place a dummy into mummy's belly button.

We have friends who have recently welcomed a newborn and he is still a bit unsure about anyone smaller than him, but I am not worrying about it as I am sure he will come around.

After all, I have enough to worry about, as you have just read.

Will you be taking paternity leave? If so, how long will you be at home?

The company I work for allows me two weeks as standard. I can then attach annual leave onto the end, but I plan on doing the same this time as I did before.

I'll have 2 weeks off once he arrives, then I'll book Mondays and Fridays as annual leave for a few weeks. We think this will be better than me being around for full weeks, as it slowly introduces my wife to looking after the children on her own. This means we are both there for four days and then she is only on her own for three.

Luckily the children have wonderful grandparents who, over the past year, have made everything so much easier by looking after Benjamin. That has allowed my wife to go back to work three days a week. They will continue to help us out once baby number two arrives.

Beth

Beth is fairly new to being a parent of two girls under the age of two. She runs a blog/book review website (www.thepiecesofme.co.uk) and is a self-employed writer.

How old was your toddler when your second baby was born?

She was a week from 20 months

How old are your children now?

Jessamy is 21 months and Lottie is nearly 6 weeks.

What was your second pregnancy like?

I was thankfully a lot less sick the second time.

Aside from that it went by fine, nothing much to report. However I was ridiculously tired towards the end which wasn't ideal with a toddler.

What was your biggest fear about having two under two? And how did you cope with the reality?

Logistics and pushing the double pram!

I dreaded trying to get them both downstairs, dressed and ready in the morning and although it's only been a few weeks I think we've almost cracked it.

Tell us about your first day coping on your own with two under two.

I panicked much more than I needed to!

Both girls were fine, although Jessamy suddenly decided she wouldn't walk up or down stairs which was helpful!

The hardest thing was keeping Jessamy entertained while I tried to feed Lottie, as she decided that was the time to open the doors and try and escape up the stairs. She's not stupid, I know that much.

What is the best thing about having two under two?

Jessamy smiling and yelling 'baba' at Lottie. It's the cutest thing and she just wants to involve her in everything.

If Jessamy is eating she tries to share with Lottie and she wants to help in every little task from settling her for sleep to changing her nappy (try and keep her hands out of that one!)

What's your top tip for coping with a baby and a toddler?

Nothing bad will happen to either of them if you leave them crying for more than 15 seconds.

Of course I don't suggest you leave a newborn wailing but sometimes if you settle your toddler it's much easier to return to your newborn – especially as you know they can't get anywhere.

I also try to make sure Jessamy has everything she needs while I'm feeding Lottie. I also try and let Jessamy be as involved as possible, watching nappy changes etc. if she shows interest.

It's still the early days for me, but I think I'm doing okay. We just need to get out more and trust that nothing bad will happen as soon as we walk out of the front door.

Which product(s) made life easier for you?

As harsh as it may seem it's one of those playpen/travel cot contraptions.

It means mornings are much easier as I can pop Jessamy in the travel cot whilst I get her breakfast sorted and Lottie is safe in her carry cot without Jessamy trying to poke her eyes out (I'm sure it's done affectionately).

How do you stay sane?

I don't! No, in all honesty I'm lucky that I have a great community of friends online who I can chat to at any time when I'm fed up of only conversing with a 20-month-old who only knows a handful of words!

Nicole

Nicole is another fantastic blogger (www.unhipnic.com). Can you tell I've met a lot of these in recent months? Her children are older than mine, making Nicole an ideal interviewee for finding out what's in store.

How old was your toddler when your second baby was born?

Lex (my son) was 20 months when Thalia (daughter) was born.

During my entire pregnancy, I read him books about babies and being a big brother. He talked to my belly. I'm not sure how much this he really understood.

The first thing he said after we picked him up from my friend's house with newborn Thalia strapped in the car seat was "What baby doing there?" Not the ecstatic homecoming I was hoping for, but he didn't seem hostile. Just really curious.

How old are your children now?

Lex is four and Thalia is two.

What was your second pregnancy like?

I would say it was easier if only because I knew what to expect. Heart attack intense heartburn? Inability to paint my toenails? Being completely convinced this was the longest pregnancy in the history of the world? Yes to all of these.

I had more nausea with Thalia than I did with Lex. My midwives attributed this to excess hormones when carrying a girl. Both my pregnancies were pretty unremarkable which I'm thankful for. They both also ended ten days past their respective due dates. I'm not so grateful for that part.

What was your biggest fear about having two under two? And how did you cope with the reality?

My biggest fear was whether they'd get along. I wish someone had told me that issue was not going to present itself for a while!

I have a sister who is six years younger than me. Growing up we never got along. The age difference was just too great. We're close now but I wish I'd had that relationship all along. I was determined to have two close together because it was important that they had each other to lean on growing up.

Lex and Thalia are great playmates now. It was hard for a while because Thalia was always too little to really play and was very clingy towards me. I did a lot of baby wearing while I played with Lex. Thalia was nearly always present so he kind of expected her to always be there.

Tell us about your first day coping on your own with two under two.

I honestly can't remember that far back. I'm not the CEO of Yahoo but I do think that babies are easy. So much easier than toddlers anyway. They stay in one place! At least for a little while.

Thalia was happy to tag along wherever as long as I or her brother was nearby. I do know that in the early days, we spent a lot of time hanging out in the big bed. Lex would help with Thalia (getting me a fresh diaper, tossing the old one) and I would praise him for being a great big brother.

He took to the role very naturally. I'm grateful for that. Maybe all those "Big Brother" books helped.

What is the best thing about having two under two?

I love watching them play together. They have incredible imaginations and watching them feed off each other as they dive deeper into their worlds is so awesome.

Lex is also a great teacher. When he noticed that Thalia was asking questions about letters, he would read books to her and point out the letters and the sounds they made.

I hope they always stay as close as they are. When Thalia is upset, she has gone to her brother for a hug. I just love that they look for each other and enjoy the other's company.

Also while they're entertaining themselves, I can do other things like cook. Or check Twitter.

What's your top tip for coping with a baby and a toddler?

Baby wearing. Wear your newborn as you chase after your toddler. It grows the bond between everyone. The toddler knows that this baby isn't going away; the baby is close to you and knows that this big kid hanging around is pretty cool too.

Which product(s) made life easier for you?

I had a Babyhawk, a mei tai style baby carrier. I loved that thing. It saved my life. It was the only way I could get anything done. I cried real tears when I parted with it.

If you could go back to those early days and tell yourself one thing, what would it be?

Relax. Also, forget about sleeping. You may remember it once upon a dream, but it's gone now and only lives in your memories. This time is hard and seems endless, but it will pass quicker than you realise.

You'll yearn for the day when a newborn slept on you and a toddler slept next you. And you'll wonder why you weren't asleep at that time too.

How do you stay sane?

What makes you so sure I am?

I make time for things that I really enjoy: photography and writing.

I run at least twice a week. Running keeps me centered.

I make sure I have 'date night' with my husband. We put the kids to bed early and watch Netflix.

I try to enjoy the little things: the way Thalia's hand feels in mine, the way Lex's eyes light up when he's learned something new and wants to share it. Things that no matter how much I try I can never truly capture in either print or photo. These things keep me happy and sane.

Made in United States
Troutdale, OR
03/03/2025

ISBN 9798733387710

90000

9 798733 387710

Journal of the Society of

Christian

Ethics

VOLUME 38, No. 2
FALL / WINTER 2018